dic·tion·ar·y | days

Also by Ilan Stavans

FICTION
*The One-Handed Pianist
    and Other Stories*

NONFICTION
*The Inveterate Dreamer
On Borrowed Words
The Riddle of Cantinflas
Spanglish
Octavio Paz: A Meditation
Bandido
The Hispanic Condition
Art and Anger
¡Lotería!*
    (with Teresa Villegas)

CARTOONS
Latino USA
    (with Lalo López Alcaráz)

TRANSLATIONS
Sentimental Songs,
    by Felipe Alfau

GENERAL
*Ilan Stavans: Eight
    Conversations*
    (with Neal Sokol)
*The Essential Ilan Stavans
Conversations with
    Ilan Stavans*

ANTHOLOGIES
*The Scroll and the Cross
The Oxford Book of
    Jewish Stories
Mutual Impressions
The Schocken Book of
    Modern Sephardic
    Literature
The Oxford Book of
    Latin American Essays
Tropical Synagogues
Growing Up Latino*
    (with Harold
    Augenbraum)
Wáchale!

EDITIONS
*Isaac Bashevis Singer:
    Collected Stories*
    (3 volumes)
*The Poetry of Pablo Neruda
The Collected Stories of
    Calvert Casey
Encyclopedia Latina*
    (4 volumes)

dic·tion·ar·y | days

A DEFINING PASSION

< ilan stavans >

Graywolf Press
SAINT PAUL, MINNESOTA

Publication of this volume is made possible in part by a grant provided by the Minnesota State Arts Board, through an appropriation by the Minnesota State Legislature; a grant from the Wells Fargo Foundation Minnesota; and a grant from the National Endowment for the Arts, which believes that a great nation deserves great art. Significant support has also been provided by the Bush Foundation; Target and Mervyn's with support from the Target Foundation; the McKnight Foundation; and other generous contributions from foundations, corporations, and individuals. To these organizations and individuals we offer our heartfelt thanks.

MINNESOTA
STATE ARTS BOARD

NATIONAL
ENDOWMENT
FOR THE ARTS

Published by Graywolf Press
2402 University Avenue, Suite 203
Saint Paul, Minnesota 55114
All rights reserved.

www.graywolfpress.org

Published in the United States of America

ISBN 1-55597-419-8

2 4 6 8 9 7 5 3 1
First Graywolf Printing, 2005

Library of Congress Control Number: 2004114974

Cover design: Kyle G. Hunter

Cover art: © Corbis. All rights reserved.

To Joan Baker,
crusader of puzzles—
with *amor*

What can be said at all can be said clearly.

LUDWIG WITTGENSTEIN
Tractatus Logico-Philosophicus, 1921

Contents

dic·tion·ar·y | days

< 1 >

Heaven

"Do words die?" asked my eight-year-old Isaiah one afternoon.

"No, they don't. They simply get stored away."

"Where?"

"In depositories . . ."

"What's a depository?"

"It's a museum. Remember the exhibit we saw about baseball in New York City? There were old cleats, Cracker Jacks, tickets, an antique radio. You liked it!"

"Yeah. It was cool!"

"Well, the exhibit used old stuff someone had taken the care to store away. And now we could all appreciate it again. You travel to the past to see how people enjoyed baseball then."

"But how can you store words? They really don't exist."

"Oh, sure they do."

"No, they don't."

"Yes. Believe me, they do."

"Where?"

"You're using them now. Aren't you?"

"But where are they?"

"How do you know what words to use?"

"I don't know. I just do."

"When you decide what to say to me, you automatically bring in the words you need. You don't even realize you're bringing them back. That is because you have many, many words stored in your memory. You've learned these words over time. Since you were little . . . you know what they mean and how to use them. Most people do."

"Is there kinof a list somewhere?"

I love how Isaiah pronounces *kinof* as if it were a single word.

"Well, not a list. The words are in your brain, one on top of the other. Or maybe they are all swimming together in a gigantic ocean. And then, when you want them, they quickly pop up. They come to you because they want to be helpful."

"But they don't have a choice. Words don't have a choice. They aren't alive."

A few seconds go by. "I don't believe it, Poppy!" Isaiah announces.

"Maybe we should ask Mom. She would know . . ."

"That's because she works with kids that have problems, right?"

"Yes, kids who have trouble pronouncing words. Or kids who cannot talk."

"Why?"

"Their mouths can't make the same sounds ours do. And sometimes the kids Mom works with have trouble remembering words."

"Do their mothers give them all the words they need?"

"I don't know. Maybe they do. And maybe sometimes they don't."

"Or perhaps their memory doesn't store words the way it should."

"That's true." I wait and then add: "Think of music. It only exists when you listen to it. Only an instrument—a violin, a piano, a flute—makes it come alive. So where is it when nobody is playing the instrument?"

"It's nowhere."

"Maybe. . . . Or maybe it's simply waiting."

"Where? In a storage place?"

"I guess."

Silence. Another few seconds go by. Then my son says: "So if everyone decides to forget a word, would that word disappear? Would it still be stored? Can words be stored forever?"

"Maybe. But at some point somebody will find them, I think."

"I'm gonna ask Mom about the museum you're talkin' about."

"Yes, you should."

Silence again.

"What's that word again, Poppy?"

"What word?"

"The word for museum? The one you used a few minutes ago?"

"I don't remember."

"Yes, you do."

"I don't, Isaiah."

"So you're forgetting words?"

"Well . . ."

Sometime later I remember. "Isaiah, do you mean *depository?*"

"Yes, *depository.*"

"Why did you want me to remember it again?"

"You know, Pop. It's kinof the same thing as a heaven."

"Who's been talking to you about heaven?"

"I just heard about it!"

"In school?"

"No."

"Where?"

"I don't remember."

"And what does it mean? What does *heaven* mean?"

"Where people go after they die."

"Mmmm."

"A depository is a kinof heaven for words," Isaiah concludes.

"I think you're right."

"It would be so cool to see that ocean, wouldn't it?"

"It would."

"But, Poppy, I don't think words exist. If nobody is playing the instrument, there is really no music. Only quiet."

< 2 >

Sleeping with My OED

Approximately a decade ago, with savings I had put aside for some time, I finally bought myself the two-volume set of *The Compact Edition of the Oxford English Dictionary*. The title says it is compact but don't be fooled: altogether the lexicon has a total of 4,116 pages and weighs some 20 pounds. Its size is equally daunting: my old wooden ruler states that it is 9½ by 12½ inches—surely not the type of compactness that makes it fit into your pocket. It won't even fit in a portfolio. Actually, I don't recommend carrying it around too much. It might break your back.

I always thought the word *compact* meant to abbreviate, to reduce in size, to make something manageable. But that is my own definition. The *OED* defines it as "to plan by compact, conspire." So what does it mean by *Compact Edition?* Maybe that the Oxford dons have conspired to make the voluminous research that went into the original edition less rowdy, more agreeable.

In any case, the two handsome volumes (*A to O* and *P to Z*) came to me stored in a blue box with a drawer on top that contains a magnifying glass. The title page states that this is the complete text of the 1971 edition and that it has been reproduced micrographically, which means that a single one of the sheets I have with me reproduces a total of four pages of the original ten-volume set of the dictionary, plus the supplement, corrigenda, and lists of spurious words and books quoted.

Known by its acronym, *OED,* this is *my* Bible. And not only mine but of 600 million English-speaking people worldwide. There are, I hasten to add, newer editions: the second edition of 1989, for instance, features 20 volumes and defines 615,100 words. These definitions include 2,436,600 quotations. The total number of words used is 59,000,000, displayed in 22,730 pages. The weight is almost 140 pounds. Needless to say, there is nothing compact about it.

There is also an online edition, immediately available—and abusable—in our rushed and jumpy age. That might be the most compact of all versions, for what is less burdensome and more elastic than the Internet?

But I care for immediacy only to a degree. Is there anything better than the feeling of an actual book in your hand, especially if it is a dictionary, and even more so if it is the *OED?* To me the pleasures of perusing its traditional format—its solid covers opening up like sanctuary doors, its delicate, almost translucent pages softening up to tactile choreography—are infinite.

This is how the *OED* describes *dictionary:*

> a book dealing with the individual words of a language (or certain specified classes of them), so as to set forth their orthography, pronunciation, signification, and use, their synonyms, derivation, and history, or at least some of these facts: for convenience of reference, the words are arranged in some stated order, now, in most languages, alphabetical; and in larger dictionaries the information given is illustrated by quotations from literature; a word-book, vocabulary, or lexicon.

Yes, the dictionary individualizes words, taking them out of context. In the "real" world, though, words behave chaotically. They pile themselves on top of each other. They defy their users in inexhaustible ways. So the dictionary does us a service: however deceitful the effort may prove to be, it attempts to bring order to chaos.

It also does something else: it tries to define *everything.* The *OED* in particular prides itself in having not left anything out. Samuel Johnson, the self-described harmless drudge, once said: "No dictionary of a living tongue can ever be perfect, since while it is hastening to publication, some words are budding, and some falling away; that a whole life cannot be spent upon syntax and etymology, and that even a whole life would not be sufficient; that he, whose design includes whatever language can express, must often speak of what he does not understand."

Johnson was an encyclopedic thinker—in today's parlance, a Renaissance man—but he also understood his own shortcomings. He knew well that no lexicon is able to grasp the universe entire. The makers of the *OED* past present and future are far more presumptuous. I'm sure they would agree with Johnson: no human effort is ever complete. They don't say so, though. Furthermore, they hide their imperfections as best they can. Now that's genius!

Still, what I like about the *OED* is precisely its attempt to defy G-d by encapsulating everything in two compact volumes—and doing so by means of exactness. That, in fact, is its best asset: the *OED* always cuts to the basics.

I'm a skeptic, too, a citizen of today's world like anyone else, and, as such, an unredeemed relativist. I know that exact is inexact, at least in this case. Exact is a synonym of accurate, but words always like to mutate. What the first Elizabethans understood as *gay* ("full of or disposed to joy and mirth") is quite different from the definition by our contemporaries, the second Elizabethans ("a male with homosexual inclinations"). Or take the word *ethnic:* to my chagrin, the 1971 edition absurdly defines it thus: "pertaining to nations not Christian or Jewish." It then adds: "Gentile, heathen, pagan." Since I arrived in the United States, I'm seen as ethnic, although (or precisely because) I'm Jewish. That is because the word today has a different meaning. So here it goes again, *ethnic:* "of or relating to a population subgroup (within a larger or dominant national or cultural group) with a common national or cultural tradition."

Anyhow, this explains why no dictionary ever compiled is absolute. It always reflects the parlance of its age and then perishes like the Sphinx tempted by fire: its knowledge becomes inexact; some words stay solid while others evaporate.

Who would I be without my *OED?* Sometimes at around 11:30 p.m., having finished the portions I had earlier left unread of the *New York Times,* I take my lexicon and browse, browse, browse. And then, rhythmically, I fall asleep with it. I envision words dancing around me. They jump out of the page, letting loose in space, intermingling with one another, making pirouettes, playing hide and seek, the letters contracting and expanding in a systole-and-diastole syncopation. Yes, words live outside our minds. They have their own private lives, filled with keenness, fervor, joy, sadness, and remorse.

I did recommend not carrying it around too much. But

I confess to doing so, day in and day out. The two volumes are seldom in their box. They might find themselves in my home office, in the bedroom, the living room, the kitchen, at times even in the porch and garden. I honestly cannot think of a book I use more often.

Its best place is near my desk. But when I lie down in bed to read, I place one of the volumes on my chest and immediately complain: too heavy!

But no sooner does the pain subside than I benefit from one discovery after another. Take the word *antipodes:* "those who dwell directly opposite to each other on the globe, so that the soles of their feet are as it were planted against each other." The definition insinuates the existence of a parallel universe to ours, a Leibnitzian reality in which the movement goes in the opposite direction from the one we're used to: up is down, east is west, light is darkness, etc. First you answer the phone and then it rings. Or else, it rains from the earth to the sky. And people are born old and grow young until they become babies. I would give my kingdom to find an antipode and chat, chat, chat.

Or take *oblat:* "a Souldier, who, grown impotent or maimed in Service, hath maintenance or the benefit of a Monks place assigned him in an Abbey." Okay, so this is a happy-go-lucky veteran. But to me an *oblat* resembles a chimera invented by Kafka, the long-lost winged rhinoceros once possessed by the Mughomami tribe in the eastern

Amazon Jungle, with a capacity to recite verbatim lost segments of the twelfth-century mystical treatise *Zohar*.

What if any one of us memorized all the words in the *OED?* It is improbable. But what if someone did? The entire memory of humankind—or at least the memory of English-speaking humankind—would be at his disposal.

In his 1967 novel *Fahrenheit 451*—the temperature at which books burn—Ray Bradbury imagines a dystopian society in which books are forbidden. His sources of inspiration are manifold. Emperor Shih Huang Ti, responsible for building the Chinese Wall, ordered the burning of all books in the kingdom. Tomás de Torquemada, Grand Inquisitor of the Holy Office in Spain (and a *converso*), also ordered the destruction of books. The list of dictators, old and new, following a similar pattern of devastation, is too long to mention. (Plus, the ignominy these tyrants deserve should include anonymity. In return for the favor, their names should be erased from memory.) But I wonder: Did any of these tyrants ever order the destruction of lexicons?

Even if they did, the memory would live on. Diderot once said: *"On ne tue pas de coups de fusil aux idées."* One might kill people but one cannot kill ideas. Lexicons are a record of our ideas as we catalogue them in the form of words.

> <

I should say that the *OED* isn't my only companion. I have a sizable collection of lexicons in my personal library, on the third floor of my house.

An aphorism comes to mind: "Tell me how you organize your books and I'll tell you who you are." Thus said a teacher of mine years ago. Then he added: "Remember: those who order their books systematically have clear thoughts."

I'm afraid I've never made the cut. In my personal library, items are organized . . . well, chaotically. Their order is ruled by sheer disorder. I shelve them as they come, intuitively, erratically. I'm the only one who ends up knowing where a single title is located. If ever I do . . .

There are two exceptions. The first is evident by looking at my volumes of *Don Quixote*. I have dozens of Spanish editions: in quarto, in octavo, critical editions, editions illustrated by Jean de Bosschere, Tony Johannot, L. Alenza, Gustave Doré, and Salvador Dalí, editions for children, etc. I also have a plethora of translations: Korean, Hebrew, French, Italian . . . they are carefully ordered. And I have reprints of seventeen different English translations. How much ink has gone into producing all these volumes?

This novel astounds me. I have endless responses to it because in a way Cervantes's narrative is an encyclopedia of human behavior. Or maybe a dictionary, one glossed in the form of adventures dealing with different human qualities.

If a classic is defined as a book whose imperfections are alleviated by the passing of time, then *Don Quixote of La Mancha* fits the bill to a T. It is, even from the viewpoint of its own author, a flawed novel: chaotic, repetitive, and stylistically inconsistent. Cervantes, at least in the first half, seems to have worked without a road map, in a haphazard fashion, unsure where to go next. Sancho Panza, for instance, an honorable poor man ("if a poor man can be called honorable") isn't even a consideration until Chapter VII, when it is clear that, in order to extract the inner thoughts of the errant knight, a Dr. Watson of sorts is needed, as companion and interlocutor, to Don Quixote's Sherlock Holmes. Elsewhere the author tells us that the original story of the errant knight, known as *The History of Don Quixote de La Mancha,* was composed in Arabic by the historian Cide Hamete Benengeli, and that Cervantes—or better, his narrator—found it in an open market in Toledo, but this device is often contradicted as the plot progresses.

Even more perplexing is the fact that Cervantes, a mediocre tax collector and soldier infatuated with his own battlefield experiences, introduces items in the narrative he later forgets about. And he embeds novellas, such as the autobiographical Moorish episode "The Captive's Tale," set partially in Algiers, and "The Novel of the Curious Impertinent," that seem to have been taken out of the drawer of "unpublished stuff" and added to the manuscript at the last minute. I'm tickled by the thought that were *Don Quixote* to debut today, it would get panned by critics.

But so what? After all, the Bible, in structural terms alone, is a considerable mess, too, and nobody seems bothered by that. In fact, that is the reason why I keep my *Quixotes* together: they remind me that imperfection can be embraced as a work of art. Part I appeared in 1605 and Part II in 1615. The initial response to them was negative: the Spanish intellectual elite was unkind. The book was either attacked or simply left unnoticed. But common readers—who in the end are always the ultimate judges— embraced it enthusiastically.

And since then, every generation approaches Cervantes's masterpiece anew, stressing the aspects it deems important and curing its imperfections by stressing their charm. For some like W. H. Auden the knight is a saint. Miguel de Unamuno believed him an endearing madman able to rise above the mendacity of the wasteland that was Spain in the seventeenth century. Unamuno even suggested that Cervantes himself was too mediocre an author to fully understand the implications of his own creation. Kafka thought Don Quixote was a dream dreamed by

Sancho. In Nabokov's eyes, this novel is the cruelest ever written. And for Milan Kundera, Alonso Quixada or Quesada, whose metamorphosis is far less theatrical than that of Gregor Samsa, is at once an antiestablishmentarian and a fatalist. Finally, for V.S. Pritchett, this amorphous piece of art "killed a country by knocking the heart out of it and extinguishing its belief in itself for ever."

Perhaps the ultimate recognition granted to an author is to turn his name into an adjective: Shakespearean, Kafkesque, Borgesian. . . . In Cervantes's case, his creation is the one that metastasizes. How do lexicons define *quixotic?* There are plenty of definitions. Take this one, for instance: "exceedingly idealistic, unrealistic and impractical." Or, in the words of the *OED:* "striving with lofty enthusiasm for visionary ideas."

The other exception in the chaos of my library is my dictionary collection. An entire wall is filled with them. These volumes seek perfection in a way that Cervantes was incapable of: they systematize knowledge. On the other hand, they are, at least partially, quixotic: they might be practical but they are also idealistic in their mission.

I have a copy of the *Encarta World English Dictionary* followed by a modern abbreviated edition of Samuel Johnson's *A Dictionary of the English Language,* released by Pantheon in 1963. My mother-in-law gave me a copy of *The New Oxford American Dictionary.* Then come a

Webster's, followed by *The American College Dictionary,* a landmark of American lexicography published in 1947 by Clarence L. Barnhart, which represents the first challenge to the supremacy of Merriam-Webster. This is followed by *The Random House College Dictionary.* My mother-in-law gave me a gorgeous copy of *The Oxford Dictionary of American Usage and Style,* also part of the collection. I have a history of Yiddish language, entitled *Geshikhte fun der Yidisher shprakh,* prepared by none other than Max Weinreich, renowned for the 1973 quote: "A language is a dialect that has an army and a navy." Weinreich is close to the *Ladino-English/English-Ladino Concise Encyclopedic Dictionary,* compiled by Elli Kohen and Dahlia Kohen-Gordon, which is seated next to similar Spanish/Arabic and English/Portuguese works. And then I have another compact edition of the portentous *Grand dictionnaire universel du XIXe siècle: Français, historique, géographique, mythologique, bibliographique, litteraire, artistique, scientifique,* etc., by none other than Pierre Larousse. (These, by the way, are side-to-side with *The Complete Merde: The REAL French You Were Never Taught at School.*)

Enough? Well, almost. ... Spanish being my mother tongue, I have an abundance of volumes in that language. Years ago I treated myself in Barcelona to a Catalan/Spanish glossary and to a Princeps edition of the *Tesoro de la Lengua Castellana o Española* by Sebastián de Covarrubias Orozco, the first so-called official dictionary of the Spanish language. I also returned home with its stepchild: a set of the *Diccionario de Autoridades,* the basis of the modern *Diccionario de la lengua española* of the Real Academia, regularly updated by a cadre of snobbish academics in Madrid. The items are next to my worn-out edition of the *Diccionario Clave,* the illustrious lexicon prepared by "the humbled housewife" María Moliner, and the two-volume *Diccionario del Español Actual,* compiled by Manuel Seco, Olimpia Andrés, and Gabino Ramos.

Yes, next to my *Quixotes* is a sea of dictionaries. . . . Why so many? I'm in the habit of collecting them the way other people collect stamps, paintings, and comic books. I have them organized by size, language and, yes, by esthetics: those with the most handsome spine are displayed where it's easiest for me to see them.

Have I always been interested in words? Not really. Up until I was twenty, my interests were sports, movies, outdoor activities. In spite of the fact that my home was multilingual, it wasn't until I left—traveling to Africa, the Middle East, Europe, and Latin America—that I became conscious of the linguistic divide that defines people. My collection is rather recent, though. For years I was penniless. The extra money I made I invested in books I felt close to. I wanted to be surrounded by them, to let myself be inspired. Mostly, I was able to afford paperbacks. I spent hours in bookstores choosing the ones I would add to my library. The history and literature sections were the sites I would always end up in. I seldom stopped by the dictionary section.

It wasn't until I had money to spare that I began to visit secondhand and antiquarian bookstores. It was then that my penchant for collecting lexicons began—and with it, my obsession to compare and contrast words.

I might be called—for lack of a better name—"a dictionary hunter" (or should it be "a dictionary haunter"?). The moment I become attracted to a dictionary, I compulsively look for ways to acquire a copy. It is difficult for me to explain what is it exactly that propels me to buy books. What's behind the business of possessing books? Why can't one simply do what is deemed normal and go to a suitable library?

The answer—as usual—is intricate. The art of collecting is intimately linked with a sense of order. One dreams of gathering in a single room a fine number of items. Their reunion might be explained metaphysically: if placed in the right proximity, these items will bring forth a sort of harmony. Plus, there is a sense of comradeship at stake as well: the conglomeration of my lexicons on a single bookshelf makes me feel at once *full* and *complete*.

These terms aren't synonymous. The fullness I experience is internal: I feel a sense of existential confidence and satisfaction. The etymological knowledge accumulated across the ages is at my fingertips. In fact, it is mine—I possess it. Conversely, the sheer presence of the dictionaries at my side grants me an external completeness: my space, the place I inhabit, is unfinished without them. And, yes, the addition of important—and unique—new items to the collection adds to that wholesomeness.

> <

Which dictionary was the first in my collection? The third edition, with supplements, of a humble one called *Appleton's New English-Spanish and Spanish-English Dictionary,* published originally in 1903. Its subtitle, centered on the page in the old-fashioned way, now seems at once portentous and ridiculous:

CONTAINING MORE THAN SIX THOUSAND
MODERN WORDS AND TWENTY-FIVE THOUSAND
ACCEPTATIONS, IDIOMS AND TECHNICAL TERMS
NOT FOUND IN OTHER SIMILAR WORK: WITH A
PRONOUNCING KEY AND THE FUNDAMENTAL
TENSES OF IRREGULAR VERBS.

My father gave it to me when I moved from Mexico to New York in 1985. Already then its brown hardcover was showing signs of overuse. He bought it when he was an adolescent and started nurturing dreams of becoming a stage actor. "I used it to read Tennessee Williams's *The Glass Menagerie,*" he once told me. "Now it's your turn . . ."

The volume still has a mark on the word *wistful*: "[uíst-full], a. *anhelante, ansioso, ávido; pensativo.—wistfully* [-i], adv. *aniosamente, ávidamente; pensativamente.—wistfulness* [-nes], s. *avidez, anhelo; estado pensativo.*"

Not too long ago, while browsing through my *Appleton's,* I returned to this definition and found out I had penciled a little smiley face in the margin next to it.

I used the *Appleton's* to read Melville's *Moby-Dick.* Six thousand words, needless to say, is next to nothing. But it was enough for me. I had come to the United States hoping to become a writer, one not only versatile in my native Spanish and Yiddish but also in English. Years before the *OED* showed up as a source of wisdom, the *Appleton's,* I'm proud to say, did the job.

I shouldn't limit my inventory of lexicons to the written page. Technology has had an impact on me, as it has on everyone else around. Day in and day out, the dictionary I go to get me quickly out of trouble—to verify the spelling of a word, to allow me a list of synonyms and antonyms— is embedded in my Microsoft Word program. Nobody will doubt that this is an utterly miraculous device: I simply pinch the section of *Tools* and an automatic lexicon, under the rubric of *Spelling and Grammar,* is available to me at no extra price and surely with no added effort. I don't even need to stand up from my desk. This device advises me by underlining misspelled words in red and by displaying syntactically incorrect portions of sentences in green. It has a thesaurus, too. And I also have a translation device (an easy click allows me to show words in Spanish, French, or English), one for hypenation, and a third for setting the program in alternative languages.

These quickies are indispensable. Who would we be without them? It is no exaggeration to say that the incorporation of electronic "word masters" into computer programs has revolutionized the way people write. The bank of words available at our fingertips makes people behave strangely. In some cases it allows for a cumbersome style. When it comes to possibilities, these lexicons, needless to say, aren't as versatile as they could be. Take the noun *neurotic*. The variants are *anxious, fearful, phobic, fixated, hung-up, disturbed, irrational, obsessed,* and *overanxious.* Neither the original noun nor its synonyms are ever defined. Hence, a browser unaware of its precise meaning won't be served well by the plethora of synonyms. In fact, these synonyms are always presented as alternatives. You might do a search to find out how often the word *neurotic* is repeated in an essay and then replace those repetitions with the variants. The result, to put it mildly, is a mess. In what context is *hung-up* a stand-in for *neurotic?*

The electronic device may push people to embrace the

ridiculous. How often have I come across, like scores of other teachers, a paper by a student with a penchant for flowery language? Once I asked a student why, out of the blue, the words *chocolate box* appeared in a sentence. In attempting to reconstruct the student's thought, I figured he was looking for an adjective like *charming* or *pleasant*. But I wasn't able to elicit a response from him. He simply offered me an innocent smile. It was only after I used my *Tools* that I found out that, for the wise makers of Microsoft Word, *charming* and *chocolate box* are synonyms.

No wonder these electronic miracles haven't made a dent in my addiction in the least for the old-fashioned dictionaries.

> <

In my collection, the *OED* is the center of gravity.

I love it for the rarities it contains. It includes the before-mentioned list of "spurious words." *Spurious* is a synonym of false, bogus, and fake. These, we are told, are words arising chiefly from "misprints and misreadings" and, as the *OED* states with its usual arrogance, the misprints "have been current in English dictionaries and other books of some authority." The majority are simply delicious. My own favorites are *abstable, beneficience, capriny, depectible, dooring, eger, hastard, investive, loudful, pailer, sardonican, scentingly, tidder, tumulate,* and *weasy.*

What do they mean? We are given definitions, although I find it more attractive to speculate on their significance. *Capriny* is a misprint of *capering,* but wouldn't it be better if it meant a type of sparkling water from Capri's hills? *Loudful* is a misreading of *loud full,* but as far as I'm concerned it should be an antonym of silent. Is a *Sardonican* a person from the now-forgotten Amazonian kingdom of Sardonica, discovered by Alonzo de Quintanilla in the sixteenth century in his journey in search of the philosophical stone? And how about *tumulate*—could it mean to get lost in a tumultuous crowd?

If given the chance, how many words could one invent and then blame on the printer? But one wouldn't need to engage in such exercise. The inventiveness of the language is, in and of itself, astounding. Scores of words go out of fashion and become relics. Who today uses the word *maraud*—to raid, pillage for plunder, to rove in search of booty? Or *rodomontade*—pretentious bragging or boasting? Or else *terpsichorean*—of or relating to dancing? The best one, I think, is *gaberlunzie*—a poor guest who cannot pay for his entertainment, a term that comes from the Scotch *gabardine* and *lunzie,* a wallet resting on the loins. "Excuse me, sir, but this restaurant has no space for gaberlunzies. So, in the most polite of fashions, please get your ass out of here!"

I'm also fond of another kind of invention, though:

evanescent words made by "those in the know" but not integral to the language, at least not in the opinion of the *OED*. Some call them *nonces. Bardolatry,* for instance, coined by Harold Bloom to describe the love of Shakespeare's work. Diana Trilling, wife of critic and Columbia University professor of English, Lionel Trilling, once described herself as "a less-educated *eclectic.*" She explained: "I don't have as many things to eclect from." And gang member Luis R. Rodriguez, author of *Always Running: La Vida Loca,* writes of *forgettery,* the condition of forgetfulness. I've also heard *doctiloquent,* to speak learnedly, and *cellephone,* an invention of Isaiah, my second son.

To eclect among nonces, think of onomatopoeic one-syllables like *oops, uh-huh, yuck,* and *boo.* Where do these expressions come from? Lewis Carroll, king of nonces, wrote thus in "Jabberwocky":

> 'Twas brillig, and the slithy toves
>> Did gyre and gimble in the wabe:
> All mimsy were the borogroves,
>> And the mome raths outgrabe.

But not all relics in the *OED* lie dormant, unused by the current generation. Words get recycled: they acquire new meanings. Take *sleepaway*—to die without disease, peaceably, and by gradual decease of the powers of nature. Fortunately, at the present time, *sleepaway* is no longer fatal, although it might be promiscuous. Or terms like *pig-Latin,* also known as *cat-Latin, dog-Latin,* and *thief-Latin,* have drastically changed their connotation. *Pig-Latin* used to imply incoherent or idle talk. Nowadays, adolescents use it to describe an invented (e.g., coded) language that idiosyncratically takes off the first sound and attaches it to the back of the word. Plus, if you start with a vowel, you add an *ay* sound at the end. Example: *Ogay otay ethay orestay*—Go to the store.

Reacting to dictionaries—feeling inspired and oppressed by them, looking for ways to emulate and deflate them—is an old sport. No wonder since, as W. H. Auden stated, writers, before anything else, are people passionately in love with language. (He really only talked about *poets,* but one should be allowed the metonymy.) Ralph Waldo Emerson spent extended stretches of time deciphering the significance of words. He, too, was an enthusiast of lexicons. I'm inspired by his quote of 1860, from "In Praise of Books," in which he attests, "Neither is a dictionary a bad book to read. There is no cant in it, no excess of explanation, and it is full of suggestion,—the raw material of possible poems and histories." The last line in particular is memorable. But Emerson's idea is only half baked: the dictionary isn't solely the raw material of future literary endeavors; and neither is it the seed of, and preamble to, those endeavors. The whole of Edgar Allan Poe's "The Raven" is in it, in scrambled fashion, and so are any of Emily Dickinson's enigmatic poems or J. D. Salinger's *The Catcher in the Rye.* And so, future masterpieces—and works of lesser relevance—are concealed in its pages, waiting to be sorted out, distilled by prospected artisans of language. Its pages are a display of art in concentrated form, ideas offered as snapshots, disconnected, abridged. The wizard whose magic unravels its conundrums is allowed the keys to an enlightened kingdom. So, yes, the dictionary is the raw material, but it contains the code to forthcoming masterpieces.

Charles Dickens was more ambivalent. In *David Copperfield,* he has the old soldier say: "What a useful work a Dictionary is! What a necessary work! The meanings of words! Without Doctor Johnson or somebody of that sort, we might have been at this present moment calling an Italian-iron a bedstead." The Briton is known to have frequented dictionaries even while on deadline, although he could also be careless and unsystematic. He was, after all, a novelist, and not one of the Joycean type. In his case, the obesity of a novel was one of its primary ingredients for success. I don't want to be Manichean in assuming that novelists (e.g., prose writers) are less infatuated with the fortunes of language while poets are more scrupulous and conscientious. "I have woven for them a great shroud," wrote Anna Akhmatova in her *Requiem* of 1940, "Out of the poor words I overheard them speak."

Vladimir Nabokov was also an aficionado of dictionaries. He claimed to keep one on his bedside table every night, although he was an insomniac also, spending the deep hours not asleep in the traditional sense of the word but dreaming away imbroglios in his studio. But does that make him friend or foe? Pablo Neruda was less ambivalent. He wrote a stunning anthem to lexicons. He called it "Ode to the Dictionary." A couple of stanzas:

> Dictionary, you are not a
> tomb, sepulcher, grave,
> tumulus, mausoleum,
> but guard and keeper,
> hidden fire,
> groves of rubies,
> living eternity
> of essence,
> depository of language.

And,

> Dictionary, let one hand
> of your thousand hands, one
> of your thousand emeralds,

a
single drop
of your virginal springs,
one grain
from your
magnanimous granaries,
fall
as the perfect moment
upon my lips,
onto the tip of my pen,
into my inkwell.
From the depths of your
dense and reverberating jungle
grant me,
at the moment it is needed,
a single birdsong, the luxury
of one bee,
one splinter
of your ancient wood perfumed
by an eternity of jasmine,
one syllable,
one tremor, one sound,
one seed:
I am of the earth and with words I sing.

My years of friendship with the dictionary have convinced me that one of its functions is to build character. I know this might seem absurd, but I believe it to be true. It is not only in the olden days that one used to hear an annoyed father announcing to his adolescent daughter: "Your foul-mouthed language is inappropriate! What you need is some intimate moments with your forgotten friend, the dictionary."

T.S. Eliot writes in *Four Quartets:*

So here I am, in the middle of the way, having had twenty years—
Twenty years largely wasted, the years of *l'entre deux guerres*—
Trying to learn to use words, and every attempt
Is a wholly new start, and a difficult kind of failure
Because one has only learnt to get the better of words
For the thing one no longer had to say, or the way in which
One is no longer disposed to say it. And so each venture
Is a new beginning, a raid on the inarticulate
With shabby equipment always deteriorating
In the general mess of imprecision of feeling,
Undisciplined squads of emotion.

Trying to learn the use of words as a means to expand one's horizon is a rite of passage: words, particularly chic, artful, sophisticated ones, bring clout. And clout is character.

For the word *character,* the *OED* offers multiple alternatives: "to engrave, imprint" and "to inscribe, write"; but also "to distinguish by particular marks, signs, or features" and "to invest." Aristotle thought that individual talent isn't an asset but a responsibility. If one has the proclivity toward composing music, it is a shame to waste one's life in something else. To build character is to delve into one's own talents, to explore their limits. Those talents, no matter what the discipline might be, need to be articulated. The dictionary enables us to accomplish that task: it gives us the tools to define and express our quest.

Plus, dictionaries like the *OED* distill authority. They are designed to shrink their browsers, to make them feel ill at ease, inept, undeserving, inferior, humiliated. The American Civil War writer Ambrose Bierce, in his *Devil's Dictionary,* a collection of sarcastic definitions that expose arrogance and corruption, aptly defines dictionary as "a malevolent literary device for cramping the growth of a language and making it hard and inelastic."

Virtually no other book—not even the Bible—emanates the same type of power and influence. Needless to say, this influence isn't metaphorical.

Or is it? There are different kinds of lexicons: intralingual and comparative, encyclopedic, etymological, historical, devoted to synonyms, to antonyms, to slang, etc. These differences might themselves be reduced to two:

normative and descriptive lexicons. The former establish the norm of a language whereas the latter limit themselves to cataloguing its variants. Both are authoritative but the former might also be accused of being authoritarian.

To put it in different terms: normative dictionaries actively tell people what the linguistic standard should be; descriptive ones take a passive role, reflecting the standard society has set.

Not that I'm in favor of one and against the other. The differences are necessary. In fact, it is crucial that both are made available to the public. This availability emphasizes the Jeffersonian quality of language, leaving it up to us to choose.

More dictionaries are published today than at any previous time in history. But are they used more often? Some experts believe it is the opposite. Every generation, at some point in time, becomes nostalgic for a long-lost past. "Ah, if people only spoke the language as they used to . . ." Or else, "Even dictionaries today are less punctilious, less precise than those of yesteryear!" The inevitable feeling is that the spoken word is—has always been—on a downhill road to perdition. Speakers today are careless about syntax, we are told repeatedly. People commit unforgivable mistakes, even sins, often unconsciously. Oh, but once upon a time, so the litany goes, our language was wholesome. Pristine and wholesome.

Really? Those exposing this theory attribute the problem to our growing illiteracy. Yes, in the industrialized world more people finish primary school today than before. But in the so-called Third World the abyss between the *knows* and the *know-nots* is more profound than it ever was. Plus, knowing the basics is no longer sufficient. Oh no, it isn't. The bank of information an average individual needs to have at his disposal nowadays in order to be functional is no doubt more substantial: mathematics, typing skills, reading fluency, medicine, geography . . .

The result is that anyone who prides himself on being literate now is more so than the equivalent person fifty years ago. The drive to become competitive in a fast-moving world, some say, has had an impact on what is taught at home and in school. People might know more today than before, but do they know it *better* than their predecessors?

Ah dictionaries! Ah humanity!

This nostalgic approach to lexicons is an illusion. In the eighteenth century, only a considerably smaller segment of society was able to read. Maybe that segment was more careful with language in general, but is that enough reason to long for a return to that less egalitarian state of affairs? This is not to say that a disheveled approach to grammar is recommended. But all ages have been simultaneously careful and careless. Dictionaries attempt to fix vocabulary, to make it immovable. But, as Johnson alerted us, it is an unattainable pursuit.

Not too long ago, I came across an interesting historical fact. I read an essay by one John Witherspoon, a Scot and a clergyman who served as president of Princeton University. Henry Louis Mencken often talks about him in *The American Language.* In 1781, Witherspoon decried that in the newly independent American Republic, people confused *eminent* with *imminent, ingenious* with *ingenuous, successfully* with *successively,* and *intelligent* with *intelligible.* Witherspoon also talked about "vulgarisms in America," such as *can't* for *cannot, don't* for *do not, knowed* for *knew,* and *winder* for *window.* Through newspapers like the *Pennsylvania Journal and Weekly Advertiser,* Witherspoon not only ridiculed these usages but attempted to correct them as well. "I have heard in this country," he wrote, "in the senate, at the bar, and from the pulpit, and see daily in dissertations from the press, errors in grammar, improprieties and vulgarisms which hardly any person of the same class in point of rank and literature would have fallen into in Great Britain." The old country clearly, in his view, was more proficient with the English language. America needed to "tighten its tongue" in order not to descend to barbarism. Witherspoon surely knew way in advance that, as George Bernard Shaw put it, "England and America are two countries separated by a common language."

Some of those barbarisms were overcome in the end, but others became accepted as part of the nation's speech. Can't open the winder? Try again until you succeed. The spoken word is so unstable, so volatile, so fickle and capricious, it isn't possible to domesticate in full. In effect, without being aware of its ephemeral nature, it domesticates us.

The authority emanating from dictionaries depends on imitation. Imitation as well as repetition. Saint Augustine recalls in his *Confessions* how he learned to speak:

I noticed that people would name some object and then turn towards whatever it was that they had named. I watched them and understood that the noise they made when they wanted to indicate that particular thing was the name which they gave to it, and their actions clearly showed what they meant, for there is a kind of universal language, consisting of expressions of the face and eyes, gestures and tones of voice, which can show whether a person means to ask for something or get it, or refuse it and have nothing to do with it. So, by hearing words arranged in various phrases and constantly repeated, I gradually pieced together what they stood for, and when my tongue had mastered the pronunciation, I began to express my wishes by means of them.

Saint Augustine was a pragmatist: he described his acquisition of nouns—table, robe, jar—but what about adjectives? For a table is never simply a table: it is also oblong, solid, beautiful, or broken. The dictionary might not teach us how to use adjectives, but at least it makes them available.

All this is to say—and apologies for the detour, but there will be more—that my *OED* is a reinvigorating artifact. I emulate it, I imitate it, I reject it . . . yet, I simply can't ignore it.

More than anything else, I attempt to read between its lines: What does it say about the scholars who put it together? And what does it think of us, its readers? Is it possible to extrapolate the philosophy of life from its thousands of definitions? What does "the Victorian behemoth," as the *OED* has been described, think about love and death? And what did it take for words like *wimmin, sexploitation,* and *microwave oven* to be included in it? Is it a manual for democracy or does it support monarchy as the most suitable form of government? Does it believe in G-d?

Nobody, to the best of my knowledge, has read it from beginning to end, a challenge that, needless to say, is not only impractical but is also not recommended. You might fall off the sofa doing it. Or worse, you literally might go out of your mind. (It is sometimes said, suspiciously, that Aldous Huxley read, page by page, almost thirty volumes of the *Encyclopedia Britannica*.) But if the enterprise were possible, I assume the questions I raised in the previous paragraphs would be answered. For no lexicographer lives outside his time: he coexists with others and responds to the exact same stimuli all of us do.

So, it's 8:30 a.m. Everyone is up. The kids are already off to school. Breakfast is over. The *OED* is in the kitchen. I've started with the *New York Times* but will leave a few sections unread until the evening. So I'm ready to begin my day. One more sojourn, I tell myself. "Fumbling for a word is everybody's birthright," Anthony Burgess wrote in *A Mouthful of Air.* I open volume *A to O.* My finger stops in the letter *M.* What kind of surprise is expecting me? My fingers slip back to *D,* then to *A.* How about *air?* How in the world would one define the word? I come across page after page of explanation: "The transparent, invisible, inodorous, and tasteless gaseous substance which envelopes the earth."

Wow, that's a mouthful. . . .

< 3 >

Ink, Inc.

A lazy afternoon.

I'm browsing through *Al-Manar*, an English-Arabic dictionary edited by Hasan S. Karmi. I wish I were more familiar with the Arabic alphabet. Fortunately, Karmi includes vowel sounds, which somewhat simplifies the task.

There seems to be an abundance of Americanisms in the selection. I pronounce alternatives of the word *faith:* دَرِين

Suddenly, I lose concentration and, boom, I'm sensible to the musicality of words. I randomly articulate a bunch, finding a rhythm through syllabication:

Ex.pres.sion
Snook
Ox.i.dize
Pic.a.resque
Co.ro.na
Noth.ing
Ma.jus.cule
Green.wich Vil.lage

Ex.e.ge.sis
Ink

The last word makes a sharp sound: ink, ink, ink. It has the quality of *onomatopoeia* ("the formation of a name or word by an imitation of the sound associated with the thing or action designated"). Onomatopoeias are based on echo: meow, whoosh, cock-a-doodle-doo, etc.

But ink doesn't echo the dancing of a pencil on the page, does it?

In the most reductive of definitions, a dictionary—and any book, for that matter—is a compendium of white sheets made from pulpwood, against which consciously organized black signs have been placed. The signs are made of ink.

Ink: from the Latin *encaustum,* the purple ink used by the Greek and Roman emperors for their signatures (thus, the term *encaustic*), used nowadays to refer to the fluid used in writing with pen on paper or parchment. And yes, it also refers to the viscous paste used for similar purposes to print a book. And it is the word that described the liquid sepia or dark brown—excreted to distract predators by most cephalopods, such as the octopus and squid, from a gland known as the ink sac near the anus.

No sooner do I utter the word yet another time than I ask: Am I pronouncing *ink* or *Inc.?*

Ah, word sounds. Yes, the sound of these two words is identical, but their meanings are galaxies apart.

Does language exist separate from sound? I, for one, strongly believe it does. Before the universe was created, every single word ever used by us, by every one of us yesterday, today, and tomorrow, was already stored in a Platonic dictionary.

Bizarrely, this theory, inspired by the work of Kabbalist Isaac Luria, shares elements with the views of the late-nineteenth-century linguist Ferdinand de Saussure in *Cours de linguistique générale* and with the work of the ultimate dissenter, Noam Chomsky, who in *Syntactic Structures* announced that language exists prior to birth, but that it acquires its grammatical shape as thought is formulated and as socialization occurs.

Thought + language = communication.

On the one hand, ink represents disorder. Spill it on the page and what do you get? An amorphous, jumbled spot—the opposite of a circle, a rectangle, or any other clearly defined geometrical pattern. In fact, the circle is to civilization what the spot is to chaos: an illustration.

By the way, in one of my lexicons, barbarism is a synonym of chaos.

On the other hand (and there are only two), ink is also literature in potential. Before the liquid is applied to the white sheet of paper, it rests quietly. But the thought and language ink will eventually become are already attached, latent, in prospective form, awaiting their future order.

So a book—and in particular a dictionary—is hence the triumph of civilization over barbarism. That, at least, is the way Michel de Montaigne used to think. Books suggest—or are supposed to suggest—organization: reason is behind them in every corner, is it not? In a single sentence, on the carefully constructed page, inside a volume seated on the shelf, in the architecture of a library.

Ink + reason = power.

Yes, ink is the stuff dictionaries are made of. It also builds bridges, neighborhoods, and habitats. It justifies codes of morality and systems of government. It inspires hatred and promotes death.

Ink ... without it, where would we be? Or better, *who* would we be? The Chinese brought ink to the West, along with powder. They formalized the journey from sound to sign. Ironically, as I look up the page in the dictionary, my attention encourages me to define its identical-in-sound counterpart: *Inc.*

> <

Inc.—always spelled with a capital *I*—isn't a mongrel word, though: it is always spelled with a dot, as in *dot-com,* for it is an abbreviation. It derives from *Incorporated,* which, the *OED* explains, is taken to mean "united into one body, combined," from the Latin *in corpore.* In the corporate environment that surrounds us, it insinuates complicity: business people grouped together with a single commercial effort in mind.

From *k* to *c* . . . is it sheer chance that has made me unite these words?

Ink is playful, whereas *Inc.* denotes consent. The former symbolizes freedom consumed by its own responsibilities, while the latter already implies what one of the consequences of those responsibilities might be. Yes, Inc. is about unity and ink about multiplicity.

I don't consider myself a troublemaker. I live harmoniously in the Capitalist environment, to the degree that is possible. At least I'm aware of—and often inflamed by— the drawbacks of a consumer society, but also appreciative of the myriad possibilities that surround me and enhance my freedom of choice. One of those possibilities is the way individualism and what I would describe as "the engine in self-drive" are promoted. Like most people I know, during the day I exist within the corporate excesses. The Cartesian *cogito, ergo sum* has been replaced by *I choose between an endless number of inanities, thus I am.*

For me the corporate world isn't an inferno but a maze

made of robots in command and robots at their service. I wholeheartedly admire those who take a less accommodating, more belligerent approach to the maze than I do. Their effort is *tragic* in the Greek sense of the term.

My resignation results in depression. I spend—or should I say *waste?*—my energy identifying and purchasing reference books because on every opportunity I have to visit a chain bookstore, I succumb to a feeling of disorientation. And disorientation gives place to dismay, which in turns becomes depression. These chains are veritable supermarkets. Everything appears to be at our disposal. But is it really?

A close look at the contents of the stores often proves the inevitable: the more merchandise we have before us, the less options we appear to have as discerning consumers. That is because the items that populate the shelves are, for the most part, commercial trash. Interesting stuff is invariably hidden where the browser might not find it.

Indeed, the reference sections I visit in chain bookstores are among the most asphyxiating. The stuff on display is banal: college dictionaries, minuscule bilingual lexicons, and a couple of humorous books on language. For corporations that make their fortunes on words, words, and words, the sight is nothing short of an embarrassment.

It isn't as if our culture disregarded etymologies. On the contrary: as a people we entertain ourselves through crossword puzzles (although not me), newspaper columns on language, books like *The Professor and the Madman* by Simon Winchester, and *Eats, Shoots & Leaves* by Lynne Truss. (The latter is a diatribe against our modern permissiveness regarding punctuation. It takes its title from a lexicographic definition of the Panda, but not from the *OED:* "a raccoon-like animal *(Ælurus fulgens)* of the southeastern Himalayas, about the size of a large cat, having reddish-brown fur and a long bushy ring-marked tail." Incidentally, why a large cat and not a small bear?) Language plays such a significant role in our daily life that some people describe us as a nation in the middle of a fateful "tongue war." Have we lost our verbal standards? Are people too liberal when it comes to syntax? Where did journalists learn to write—or better, did they ever learn? Why are adjectives so abused today (it was the philologist Raimundo Lida who said once, "Adjectives were made not to be used")? Unfortunately, a person in need of answers will not find satisfaction in the reference section of the local chain, for the lack of respect for books in these so-called Temples of Knowledge is obscene.

Not only obscene but obnoxious, too. How often have I stopped at an information desk to ask for advice and the reply I get from the clerk is *ugh!,* an onomatopoeia even the dictionary finds troublesome to spell. Books happen to be on sale at these stores, but the items might just as well be

Q-tips. (Yes, I wrote *Q-tips,* the slim cotton sticks used for cleaning the auditory orifices. In its arrogance, the *OED* is oblivious to this and other corporate brand names.)

I didn't intend for this section to become an indictment of corporate America, though. Is too much merchandise bad for one's health? Truth is, I don't know. Or better, I really don't care.

Ink + Inc. = powerlessness.

> <

Nightfall.

Again I invoke the first equation: thought + language = communication.

Al-Manar is still on my lap. I put it aside and reach for a book on the shelf. It is a small volume by Samuel Beckett on Proust. It includes a series of three dialogues with Georges Duthuit, an art critic with whom Beckett occasionally played chess in Paris cafés in the 1940s and with whom he debated the nature of art and the painters who were in vogue at the time. In one of these conversations, Beckett reflects on the loss of meaning in the contemporary world, a favorite topic in his oeuvre. He categorically states that

there is *nothing to express,* nothing with which to express, nothing from which to express, no power to ex-

press, no desire to express, together with the obligation
to express.

The endearing sentence, with its well thought-out ink
patterns, is easily understandable. Somehow it makes
me think of Miles Davis's jazz variations. Beckett infuses
his language with a syncopated rhythm: *** stop *** stop
*** stop, followed by a change of movement as the word
obligation is approached, then impeded by the word
express.

I think of "Deathfugue" by Paul Celan, a poem about
the Holocaust and the end of poetry. In it an orchestra
of Jewish musicians plays a violin arrangement—a piece
called "Death Tango" —as people march, dig their own
graves, and are then killed by the Nazis:

Black milk at daybreak we drink it at evening
we drink it at midday and morning we drink it at night
we drink and we drink
we shovel a grave in the air there you won't lie too cramped
A man lives in the house he plays with his vipers he writes
he writes when it grows dark to Deutschland

Expresso—is this what Beckett and Duthuit are drinking
while they talk, I wonder? There is nothing like a strong

dose of caffeine to let the mind loose. Or is he after the elusive concept of *expression,* "the action of pressing or squeezing out"? And what about *nothing,* to which, given its self-contradictory meaning ("a non-existent thing"), the *OED* devotes almost three full pages?

Ink, Inc.

< 4 >

No-Kim-Bah

I had a dream several nights ago.

It was around 11:30 p.m. I was in bed browsing my *OED* when I fell asleep. Or maybe I simply entered that most inspiring realm where our senses are still active yet reason has receded and our imagination has taken full command.

I'm walking inside a Middle Eastern market. Vendors display fruit, condiments, vegetables, utensils, jewelry, videos, and CDs. . . . There's a hoopla: someone has been robbed.

"A thief! A thief!" I turn around and see people running after an adolescent. But they can't catch him. One says: "Ah, there goes another bastard. If parents aren't responsible, whom should one blame?"

I reach a stand where books are sold. The merchant is sitting down on a stool in a corner, listening to the radio. A soccer game is taking place somewhere. He smiles at me.

There's an elongated table in front of me. On top of it I see several dozen volumes, maybe a hundred. Most look rather disheveled. They are organized by color: lavender, fuchsia, maroon, orange, auburn, and yellow. I take up one and look at it carefully. It is decorated with golden ornaments stamped against a green background. The spine says: *Lisan al-'Arab*. I open it up. It is by Abdul Fadl Muhammad bin Mukarram. I browse through its pages, then put it back in order to glance through a few more: *Al-Mufridat Gharib al-Qur'an* by Abdul Qasim ar-Raghib. I also see *Taj al-'Urus* by Murtada az-Zabidi and *Muhit al-Muhit* by Patras Bustani.

I take a step back and head for another selection near the far left corner of the stand. I open a volume that has an epigraph by Joseph Conrad: "My task which I am trying to achieve is by the power of the written word, to make you hear, to make you feel—it is, before all, to make you *see*. That—and no more, and it is everything." Then I read through another one. It's also in Arabic, written by a certain Benegueli or Benengel (I can't make out the letters). My fingers stop on page 12. "*Al-Baqarah*." I read further:

> *Alif lām mīm*
>
> This is The Book free of doubt and involution,
> a guidance for those
> who preserve themselves from evil
> and follow the straight path,

Who believe in the Unknown
and fulfill their devotional obligations,
and spend in charity
of what We have given them;

Who believe
in what has been revealed to you
and what was revealed to those before you,
and are certain of the Hereafter.

They have found the guidance of their Lord
and will be successful.

As for those who deny,
it is all the same if you warn them or not,
they will not believe.

God has sealed their hearts and ears,
and veiled their eyes.
For them is great deprivation.

I also return this book to the table and find yet another
attractive book:

All of them entered ... and found more than a hundred
great volumes, and those very well bound, besides the

small ones. And as soon as the old woman had seen
them, she departed very hastily out of the chamber, and
soon returned with a great speed, with a holy-water pot
and a sprinkler in her hand, and said: "Hold, master
licentiate, and sprinkle this chamber all about, lest there
should lurk in it some one enchanter of the many which
these books contain, and cry quittance with us for the
penalties we mean to inflict on these books, by banish-
ing them out of this world."

I hear the vendor say: "Ar-Rahman . . . beware of the
enchanter."

I look up. But he's still hooked to the radio! I'm overwhelmed by the urge to steal one of these books. Which
one? I select a lavender one. Before I take off, I decide to inspect it. Ah, but its pages are entirely empty. Mmm . . . how
can that be? I look at the rest of the books on the table, even
the ones I already browsed. None of them contains anything written, neither inside nor on the cover or spine. The
vendor looks up. He says: "They have no stories. Nothing.
No, no stories, sir."

I'm puzzled. But I had seen . . .

"No stories," he repeats. "Nothing."

"So . . . what do they say?"

"They say nothing. They're for the senses. The senses.

These books contain aromas. Smell. Go ahead, smell. Smell the one you're holding in your hands."

It smells of spine. "Juniper, eh?" the vendor says. "Now close your eyes."

I comply. Gradually I feel as if transported into a desert. Around me I see dryness. Nearby are cacti. Under a rock I see a lizard's tail. I sense the penetrating smell of juniper everywhere. In a canyon in Arizona, I once bought from a Navajo girl a piece of petrified wood and a box of incense. Her face comes back to my mind. I remember that she spoke no English. I wondered then: Are there dictionaries of Navajo? After I gave her a $10 bill, she placed her right hand under her shirt and took out a bottle. "For hair," she said. "Makes head sane, señor."

I don't understand her. The bottle appeared to contain shampoo of some sort. But was it?

"Is it shampoo?"

"*No-kim-bah, no-kim-bah.*"

"What is '*no-kim-bah*'?"

The aroma of juniper evaporates and I'm overwhelmed by a terrible headache.

Do words have color? Do they have flavor? How about smell? Yes, I think to myself. Words do have smell. Language has smell.

No, it doesn't, I tell myself. It is difficult to remember

smells. Can a dog remember the smell of meat? I don't know. We are able to invoke data, images, and sounds. Maybe we also remember sensations. But not smells.

But do language and smell go together? The books I have at home also have a smell. "Oh, come on! Do they really?" I hear myself ask. *Madame Bovary*—what does it smell of, the nineteenth-century French provincial town of Rouen?

I don't know why but at this point the word *maelstrom* comes to me. I let my lips stretch its syllables—*ma-el-strom*—and taste its Scandinavian origin.

"Thirty-five shekels."

The headache intensifies. "Thirty-five . . . wake up, Mister!" the vendor shrieks. "Thirty-five. Thirty-five shekels."

Should I run? My heartbeat accelerates rapidly.

> <

Alison, my wife, suddenly wakes me up. "Ilan, you're snoring. You're not letting me sleep!"

< 5 >

Pride and Prejudice

In *The Dyer's Hand and Other Essays,* W. H. Auden writes:

> Though a work of literature can be read in a number
> of ways, this number is finite and can be arranged in a
> hierarchical order; some readings are obviously "truer"
> than others, some doubtful, some obviously false, and
> some, like reading a novel backwards, absurd. That's
> why, for a desert island, one would choose a good dic-
> tionary rather than the greatest literary masterpiece
> imaginable, for, in relation to its readers, a dictionary
> is absolutely passive and may legitimately be read in
> an infinite number of ways.

But what dictionary? For each culture has the dictionaries
it deserves. Dictionaries are like mirrors: they are a reflection of the people who produced and consumed them.

Let me start with an open landscape. The roots of lexicography go back to . . . when? Probably to the non-Semitic
cultures (Acadians, Sumerians, etc.), to whom we owe such

fossils as the *Epic of Gilgamesh*. Even before the appearance of ink as we know it ("the coloured fluid [usually black] ordinarily employed to writing with a pen on paper, parchment, etc."), cuneiform was used to communicate the plight of a folk hero. And cuneiform was also employed to decode the language used to narrate the hero's epic.

The profession makes its true arrival in Sanskrit. Then the γλωσσογραφοι, the Greek *glossographi,* were commissioned to explain Homer and other classic authors to the public. In works like Aristophanes's *The Birds,* various dialects are juxtaposed. The play reads:

> INFORMER: Just give me wings.
> PEISTHETAERUS: That's exactly what I am doing, by
>   talking to you like this.
> INFORMER: How can words give a man wings?
> PEISTHETAERUS: Words can give everybody wings.

An apparatus pointing to the connections a passage had to other aspects of culture was devised. The word to describe these artifacts is *concordance.* The *OED* defined it as "the fact of agreeing or being concordant." And then: "a treaty, agreement, or compact." Concordances showed up in Attic or Doric to contextualize, to offer a sense of connectedness, first in theater, then in poetry. And what's a concordance if not a dictionary?

If historians have it right—and they often don't—the first true dictionary was the *Lexeis*. It appeared around 200 BCE, compiled by another Aristophanes: Aristophanes of Byzantium. Unlike modern lexicons, its approach was by class, organizing references together according to their hierarchy in the universe. (It's really more like *Roget's Thesaurus*.) In the Roman period, Marcus Terentius Varro is worthy of mention for his *De Lingua Latina* (*circa* 80 BCE), an attempt to examine the Latin grammar and syntax, and also a record of numerous etymologies.

Arabic lexicography is also important (and often ignored). I have made it a priority in my intellectual quest. The *Kitāb al-'Ain,* inconclusively attributed to al-Khalil ibn Ahmad and considered the forerunner of modern Arabic dictionaries, appeared in 862–3 CE. The volume set out to catalogue the roots—though not the words—of the Arabic language. Organized anagrammatically, it contains twenty-six chapters, one for each of the letters of the alphabet, with the exception of the weak ones. Ibn Ahmad was followed by, among others, Abū Bakr ibn Duraid, whose lexicon *Jamharat al-lugha,* published around the year 915, sought to legitimize Arabic as a literary language. Ibn Duraid wrote a preface that ought to be read as a plea for literacy in the Islamic world in particular, and as a *raison d'être* of sophisticated glossaries in general:

When I saw the neglect of literature of the people of this generation, their reluctance to learn, their hostility to what they do not know, their loss of what they have been taught; when I saw that the noblest of God's gifts to his creatures is breath of knowledge, the power to discipline themselves, intelligence with which to restrain their passions; when I saw the mature man of our time, though the domination of stupidity over him, and the stranglehold of ignorance, loosing what the past has bequeathed him, circumscribed in his notion of his obligation; so that it is as if he is but the son of his own day, and the offspring of his own hour; when I saw the rising generation, though capable and gifted, preferring pleasures, and turning from paths of virtue . . . I stored up strength, talked to learned men, and arranged this dictionary according to alphabetical order, as being more comfortable to people's knowledge, and more attuned to their ears. So if anyone consults this book and wants to find a bilateral expression, let him begin with the *hamza,* then the *bă,* if the second letter is a heavy *bă,* then the hamza and the *tă,*" and so on.

The Middle Ages saw an outpouring of Latin, English, and French glossaries. The need to establish a bridge between the language of intellectual discussion used in monasteries and more earthly tongues was the engine that set lexicography in motion. Among the most significant was the *Dictionarium ex optimis quibusque authoribus studiose collectum. . . .* Published in 1502, it was executed by the Augustan monk Ambrosius Calepinus (who, by the way, was blind, just like Homer). Over time the Calepinus became a standard oeuvre in erudite circles. Its appeal is to be found in its polyglotism: in one of its latter editions—it was reprinted and updated often—it included a total of eleven languages, including German, Spanish, English, Hebrew, French, and Latin.

Ah, the languages of the world in a single volume!

Interestingly, multilingual lexicons appeared to have established their marketability before single-language ones. Not long ago, at the Folger Library in Washington, D.C., I was allowed to browse through John Baret's ambitious dictionary of 1573, known for its elephantine title (utterly unmarketable in today's culture): *An alvearie or triple Dictionarie: in Englishe, Latin, and French: very profitable for all such as be desirous of any of those three languages. Also by the two tables in the ende of this booke, they may contrariwise, finde the most necessary Latin or French wordes, placed after the order of an alphabet, whatsoever are to be founde in any other dictionarie: and so to turne them backwardes againe into Englishe when they reade any Latin or French aucthors, & doubt of any harde worde therein.* And I also perused Sieur Guy Miege's *Nouvelle methode pour*

*apprendre l'anglois. Avec une nomenclature, françoise & an-
gloise, un recueil d'expressions familieres, et des dialogues,
familiers & choisis,* made available more than a hundred
years later. During the same occasion, I opened one of
Shakespeare's quartos and a first edition of Dr. Johnson's
A Dictionary of the English Language. The pleasure that
comes from having these items in hand is indescribable.
The word *sublime* ("set or raised aloft, high up") is the
most appropriate: I felt elevated, closer to the heavens. I
remember my heart palpitating rapidly as I opened them. I
felt transported to the past—to sixteenth-century London.
But I was also aware of the historical awareness that made
me sensitive to the volumes. In other words, as my mind
meandered, past and present were . . . well, concordant.

In any case, between these two items, one British,
the other French, a plethora of imitations came into being, designed to satisfy the curiosity of an age defined by
incipient transcontinental journeys. Imitation, let it not
be forgotten, is the most repeated of mental activities, to
the extent that it often becomes a trap. The enthusiasm
these compendiums generated was infectious. It became
a philosophical mission by the French Encyclopædists
(Diderot, Voltaire, et al), whose aspiration it was to turn
the mind into the ultimate tool of control. I'm still in
awe of their motives. Theirs was an implausible dream:
to organize and register all aspects of human knowledge

accumulated until then, from the plain and simple to the most elaborate. In order for the enterprise to be successful, nothing—absolutely nothing—could be left out: a pebble, an inkwell, coffee, horses, fingernails, the color blue, hatred, the theater, servitude, the giraffe's neck, the future tense.... Did the Encyclopædists ever doubt themselves? Of course, doubt—"the (subjective) state of uncertainty with regard to the truth or reality of anything; undecidedness of belief and opinion"—was an integral part of the venture, but it was never an obstacle. Instead, in Diderot in particular, it was a stimulus. And did they, quixotic in their approach, fear being accused of being foolish? Again, yes: yet they knew, in their wisdom, that there isn't an intellectual effort that is not, at its core, subject to ridicule. For the intellect itself plays always with artifice, and artifice is a "human skill as opposed to what is natural." For how on earth would one be so ambitious, so "strong-minded"—the adjective is exemplary—if not by daring to accomplish the absurd: to delineate, with as much accuracy as possible, not only G-d's map but His language, too?

Today there are dictionaries of Aramaic, ballet, gerontology, hip-hop, knighthood, Napoleon's wars, proteins, Russian slang, and TV. Browse the catalogue web page of the Library of Congress and allow yourself to be flabbergasted. The search stops at 9,976 references, advising, nauseatingly, that this is but a fraction of the total. That total is as voluminous as it is diverse. It even contains a Slovenian dictionary of silence, composed by one Ales Debeljak.

> <

Since my collection of lexicons is especially strong on Anglo-Protestant and Hispanic-Catholic items, I will focus on these two specific cultures. How different are their traditions? Are their divergent ways symbolic of larger cultural patterns?

The early practitioners of the Anglo-Protestant tradition were often penniless editors. They managed to practice their passion outside universities and published their lexicons with the help of subscribers. Their names are Robert Cawdrey (*A Table Alphabeticall of Hard Usual English Words,* 1604), Henry Cockeram (*The English Dictionarie: or, An Interpreter of Hard English Words,* 1623), Thomas Blount (*Glossographia: or, a Dictionary Interpreting all such Hard Words . . . as are now used in our refined English Tongue,* 1656), Stephen Skinner (*Etymologicon Linguae Anglicanae,* 1671), Elisha Coles (*An English Dictionary,* 1676), John Kersey the Younger (*A New English Dictionary,* 1702), and Nathan Bailey (*An Universal Etymological English Dictionary,* 1721). And then, arriving almost as a messianic figure, comes Samuel Johnson. His foundational views on lexicography set the pattern for generations to come.

In August 1747, Dr. Johnson published his *Plan of a Dictionary of the English Language,* which, for political and financial reasons, he addressed to the Earl of Chesterfield. His objective was to fix the language: to cleanse it of French (and to a lesser extent, American) terms, to standardize its vocabulary, and—herein his revolution—to offer historical quotes from major English authors defining their usage. Johnson's *A Dictionary of the English Language* appeared in 1755, nine years after he signed a contract based on his original plan. It is not only the most erudite and authoritative lexicon produced by a single set of hands, but also the wittiest and most entertaining one I've ever come across. Johnson does what no other etymologist dares to: he is sarcastic. His sarcasm is found in his view that lexicons are not only verbal registers but—lo and behold!—artistic statements on human nature and world affairs. He perceived his task to be a battle between darkness and light, between reason and distress. He believed that "things may be not only too little, but too much known, to be happily illustrated." Johnson was, unquestionably, a social commentator, an interpreter. "The rigour of interpretative lexicography," he announced in his preface, "requires that the explanation, and the word explained, should be always reciprocal."

And what about the other side of the Atlantic?

The Founding Fathers of the American Republic, in

particular John Adams, planned to safeguard the essence
of English. Adams believed an Academy ought to be established, as H. L. Mencken put it, to, among other things,
"pass on the merits of new words." In general, its duty
would be the advocacy "for refining, improving and ascer-
taining the English language" in America. In 1774, in the
Royal American Magazine, writing under the pseudonym
of Aristarcus, Adams suggested the appointment of
Fellows of the American Society of Language, a predeces-
sor of sorts to the American Academy of Arts and Sciences,
a non-federal institution established four years later, which,
happily, refuses to take responsibility for the well-being of
English in the United States. Six years later, he wrote letters
to Congress recommending the formation of an academy
that would protect the English language from a slow process of deterioration and maybe even destruction. He believed this needed to be done because in the long run
English would come to conquer the world. "This I should
admire," Adams wrote:

> England will never more have any honor, excepting
> now and then that of imitating the Americans. I as-
> sure you, Sir, I am not altogether in jest. I see a general
> inclination after English in France, Spain and Holland,
> and it may extend throughout Europe. The population

and commerce of America will force their language
into general use.

In the nineteenth century, Noah Webster relocated the
center of gravity of English-language lexicography. He first
published the best-selling *American Spelling Book.* Then,
in 1828, he came out with his *American Dictionary of the
English Language,* which was an attempt to legitimize the
colonial tongue. Webster based his research almost exclusively on the language of New Englanders. But he also made
use of much of Johnson's databank. In fact, Webster was at
times accused of plagiarizing Johnson. But when Joseph
Worcester's *Comprehensive Pronunciation and Explanatory
Dictionary of the English Language* appeared in 1830, Webster himself accused Worcester of the same sin.

The two of them, Webster and Worcester, were followed
by Charles Richardson's *A New Dictionary of the English
Language,* which emphasized quotations as etymological
substitutes for standard lexicographic definition. So, on
both sides of the ocean, the effort of free-enterprising
individual lexicographers made it possible for the English
language to delineate its possibilities.

But unquestionably the most important dictionary in
the English language, and arguably the biggest contribution
of all time, is the *Oxford English Dictionary,* my favorite.

Its history has been chronicled, in superb form, by Simon Winchester in his book *The Meaning of Everything* from a panoramic perspective, and in a more personal tone by Katherine Maude Elisabeth Murray, granddaughter of the primary compiler of the lexicon, in *Caught in the Web of Words.*

Its origins date to 1842, when an Oxfordshire dweller by the name of Edwin Guest established the so-called Philological Society. This club manifested its displeasure with the dictionaries available at the time and commissioned a report to list the important English words that had been left out. The idea was then introduced to embark on a lexicographic effort—eventually called *The New English Dictionary*—that would attempt to become the most comprehensive dictionary ever published.

Little did the members of the Philological Society suspect that such a project would take an amount of energy no other etymological endeavor had ever received, and that so lengthy and tedious would the project be that the people designated as editors would come and go. These editors would include Herbert Coleridge, Frederick James Furnival, both of whom had been original members of the Philological Society. Eventually the dictionary would fall in the lap of the Oxford dons. It all began in 1884. The project was variously called *New English Dictionary on Historical Principles,* then *Oxford English Dictionary,* and *Murray's Dictionary.* By far the most push came from James August Henry Murray, who saw to it that the effort would be completed. Murray believed that

> the Vocabulary of a widely-diffused and highly-cultivated living language is not a fixed quantity circumscribed by definite limits. That vast aggregate of words and phrases which constitutes the Vocabulary of English-speaking men presents, to the mind that endeavors to grasp it as a definite whole, the aspect of one of those nebulous masses familiar to the astronomer, in which a clear and unmistakable nucleus shades off on all sides, through zones of decreasing brightness, to a dim marginal film that seems to end nowhere, but to lose itself imperceptibly in the surrounding darkness.

It would happen one slow volume at a time and would not start until the century was already at a close, in 1897. In its complete form, it would see the light in 1928, almost ninety years after its inception.

After the *OED* consolidated its place, the number of lexicons available to the public (*Merriam-Webster, American Heritage, Random House* ...) has not diminished. Today lexicography is accomplished electronically. Research depends on a scientific approach to etymology and on thousands of correspondents worldwide. Some of the *joie de vivre* might have been lost.

> <

Conversely, Hispanic-Catholic epistemology was set for years not in the recording and systematizing of the Spanish language as a whole, but in the cleansing of it from the excesses it "fell victim to" in its contact with foreign—i.e., unwelcome—forces.

The year 1492 is known, sarcastically perhaps, as the *annus mirabilis* of Hispanic civilization: Granada capitulated and Boabdil was thrown into exile; Jews were finally expelled by the Catholic monarchs, Isabella of Castilla and Ferdinand of Aragón, from the Iberian Peninsula; some three months later, Columbus arrived in the Bahamas; and, contemporaneously with these two cathartic events, Antonio de Nebrija at the University of Salamanca published the first Castilian grammar.

Prior to Nebrija, Spanish was one more of the several unruly languages of the Iberian Peninsula, which, as it happens, would remain attached to a feudal system until late in the eighteenth century. The Catholic kings had succeeded in what is known as *La Reconquista*, the unification of Spain under a single banner: one religion, one language, one government. In retrospect, it appears that Nebrija was responsible, to a large extent, for making Spanish a unifying force. And it was he who, in his grammar, described this language of poets like Gonzalo de Berceo, Juan Ruíz Arcipreste de Hita, and Jorge Manrique, as "a companion of empire," thus declaring it the official tool in the colonial quest of the Americas. Thanks to the conquistadors and missionaries, Spanish became the instrument of control of the aboriginal population across the Atlantic.

Between 1492 and 1496, a number of dramatic changes took place in Spanish culture, significantly the dialogue with the newly encountered Americas. Not surprisingly, Nebrija registered the earliest Americanism in a European lexicon: the word *balsa,* craft (usually made of hollowed tree trunks), appears in his grammar of 1492, yet four years later it is replaced by the Nahuatl voice *canoa,* canoe. Incidentally, according to Mencken, the word *canoe* was "picked up from the Indians of the West Indies by Columbus's sailors as a Haitian word." Together with maize—in Spanish *maíz,* corn—it appeared in English for the first time in 1555, although it was spelled then as *canoa.* It eventually came to describe a native vessel operated by paddles.

Nebrija's successor was the Inquisitorial Sebastián de Covarrubias, whose *Tesoro* appeared in 1611, almost exactly in between the release of the first and second parts—1605 and 1615, respectively—of Cervantes's *Don Quixote of La*

Mancha. Covarrubias offered a more complete, if also religiously partial, dictionary of the Spanish language. Covarrubias was a priest of the Holy Office of the Inquisition. His lexicon was published with the imprimatur of that intolerant institution, and not surprisingly, its definitions were tailored to represent the views supported by the church.

Take, for example, the word *judío,* Jew in Spanish. Herein a partial quote:

> *En la palabra hebrea tenemos dicho en qué forma aquel pueblo, que Dios escogió para sí, se llamaron hebreos y después israelitas, y finalmente judíos. Hoy día lo son los que no creyeron en la venida del Mesías Salvador, Cristo Jesu, Señor nuestro, y continúan el profesar la ley de Moisés, que era sombra desta verdad.*

Translation:

> In the Hebrew word we have the way in which that people, which God chose for Himself, were called Hebrews, then Israelites, and finally Jews. Today they are the ones that didn't believe in the coming of the Redeeming Messiah, Jesus Christ, Our Lord, and continue to profess the Mosaic Law, which was a shadow of that truth.

Yes, no dictionary, at any point in time, is entirely objective. Plus, dictionaries make mistakes. And each culture, without exception, produces lexicons colored by bigotry. But few nations make those lexicons the centerpiece of their verbal tradition. It isn't surprising that Covarrubias's infamous *Tesoro* was popular in its time. But it is sorrowful that this *Tesoro* would be canonized in the centuries to come, its definitions plagiarized and reshuffled time and again. Along with its counterparts produced under the Soviet regime and other systems, it is less a reference source than an instrument of hatred.

> <

As time went by, the paths of these two cultures, Anglo-Protestant and Hispanic-Catholic, became even more emphatically divergent.

The key item pushing them apart was the different approach to institutionalization that each would take. Spanish joined other European languages (French and Italian) in embracing a path defined by government support, whereas English chose an alternative route defined by government independence.

In Florence and France, academies were established in the sixteenth and seventeenth centuries to uphold the dignity and continuity of Italian and French as national tongues: the Accademia della Crusca, the first of its kind, appeared in 1582 and was devoted to maintaining Italian culture; the Académie française was established in 1635, and it also modeled its mission in patriotic terms. (Flaubert said of it: "Run it down, but try to belong to it if you can.") The *Vocabolario della Crusca* was published in 1612 and the *Dictionnaire de l'Académie française* was released in 1694.

Always late to jump on board, the Spanish would follow suit not long after, consolidating their own Real Academia Española in 1713. One of the objectives of the Spanish Academy was the publication of a lexicon of the caliber of the French one. Its members embarked on the project. It took them fourteen years—from 1726 to 1740—to produce the *Diccionario de Autoridades.*

The lack of an open, entrepreneurial spirit has been a stigma of Hispanic civilization. Traditionally, democracy has had trouble establishing itself as a system of government. Not surprisingly, the deeply rooted dogmatism from Spain projected itself onto the colonies across the Atlantic. Each of the nations in the Americas that once were connected to Spain had its own branch of the Real Academia Española. To this day the lexicon regularly published in the Iberian Peninsula is disseminated in the Spanish-speaking world as if it were the word of the prophets. For better or for worse, Mexico, Colombia, Argentina,

Peru ... these countries continue to see Madrid as the apex of verbal correctness.

It was the romantic spirit that brought about this change. Nationalism was in the air. Countries were looking to define themselves as units vis-à-vis their neighbors. Language, clearly, was understood to be a collective treasure. That treasure might be in peril as a result of natural forces. It might lose its consistency, it might borrow too much from outside tongues, and it might descend into chaos if a standard spelling system were not established. The defense of the language was put in the hands of an intellectual elite. There was enthusiasm for this approach but also skepticism. Moliére said in 1673: "Once you have the cap and gown all you need to do is open your mouth. Whatever nonsense you talk becomes wisdom and all the rubbish, good sense."

England and its colonies—and, in particular, what would become the United States—didn't follow suit. At various points in history the question of *why not?* has popped up. Supporters of the idea surely pushed for it, among them Daniel Defoe, Jonathan Swift, and, later on, Matthew Arnold. But their immodest proposals led nowhere. I say *happily* because, at the dawn of the twenty-first century, it is clear today more than ever that English has not only survived the apparent benefits of a federally funded institution in charge of defending the language, but it has also thrived with ferocious candor without the help of any federal institution.

As a Mexican native and a Spanish speaker, I have endless qualms with the Real Academia Española in Madrid. The entity still uses a slogan dating back to its inception: *limpia, fija y da esplendor*—clean, fix and grant splendor. In the age of colonialism, such a maxim partially made sense. But relativism is a *sine qua non* today. The world has drastically changed in the last two hundred years. What does "grant splendor" mean in our current context—the power and beauty of Spanish at the expense of what? Fix is a more acceptable term. Yet by far the most troublesome is *clean*. In fact, an adequate translation might also use the word *cleanse*. Mmmm: cleanse from what? Language is freedom. It needs artists, scholars, and educators. It doesn't need police.

Unparalleled routes. The *OED* is the product of a private enterprise: Oxford University. It exerts authority by virtue of its richness and scope. The *Diccionario de la lengua española,* instead, is a government-produced artifact. It is designed to legislate the Spanish language, thus inhibiting its growth.

Language encourages progress, or handcuffs it. Language showcases the pride of a culture—in Dr. Johnson's words, "a nation's pedigree"—but also confirms its prejudices.

< 6 >

Fictionary: *or, How I Learned to Write*

Reading, reading, reading . . .

For some, reading leads to writing. In my case, it was the other way around. I'm a feisty, voracious reader. I read from dawn to dusk: books, newspapers, magazines, manuals, brochures, you name it. I read anything that crosses my path. As I mature—is the grey hair an omen?—I find myself rereading more. I return to favorite novels of another time, stories and poems I discovered years ago. I delve into their pages afresh and memorize a poignant line, reacquaint myself with a plot long forgotten, and reevaluate the depth of a favorite character.

Surprise, surprise. The definitions for *reading* offered by the *OED* are nothing if not convoluted. The first, an obsolete one, states that *read* is "the fourth stomach of a ruminant." Then it says: "to have an idea, to think and suppose." Later: "to make out or discover the meaning or significance of (a dream, a riddle, etc.)." In my eyes the best one, though, is "to foresee, foretell."

Reading is all those things and more. It is an act of

reason, an attempt to decipher the mysterious universe that houses us. But when I was an adolescent, reading was a chore. I found little pleasure in it. Books were common in my parents' home but I had little interest in them. Instead, images were my absolute passion. To this day I'm unable to remember names but I can store images (faces, landscapes, textures . . .) instantaneously. I wanted to be a filmmaker because I formulated my ideas in images. And so I loved movies. Maybe *love* is too weak a word: I was anesthetized by them. I even thought of my life—my past, especially—as a movie. In the age before videos and DVDs, my father, an actor and another film freak, regularly took me to see films several times a week. We saw as many new releases as possible and also frequented rerun houses where classics were shown.

My passion for images was, in some way, a response to my allergy to writing. I knew that if I wanted to tell a story on the silver screen I needed to write it first. But I procrastinated as much as possible because I was ashamed of it. My problem: I was a terrible speller. No matter what language I wanted to write in, on the page words were eternally unstable. Would I ever remember their shape?

In retrospect, the way I ended up solving the problem makes it look simple. When I write a sentence now, I'm able to visualize the words—I feel I can even touch them—a hundredth of a second before they are marked down on the page. And if I can visualize them, I can also spell them. I've turned each and every one of them into images I've committed to memory. Over the years I've made a verbal bank in my mind, from where I deposit and withdraw at will. This is the case in all the tongues I know: every one of them has its respective reservoir. These reservoirs never get mixed up—unless, that is, I deliberately want them to.

Nobody is born with ready-made verbal banks. At most we're endowed at birth with an internal mechanism enabling us to store information. But the reservoirs themselves are the product of education.

My father would be impatient with my spelling problem. He used to tell me that the moment I finally found my way around words, I would think more clearly. He insinuated that a universe ruled solely by images was an impoverished place unworthy of us. I didn't understand what he meant until I decided to write my first screenplay.

By then I was at the *Yiddishe Schule in Mexique,* a private Yiddish middle school. Somehow I had managed to navigate through one grade after another without doing much writing. One day one of my Spanish-language teachers, to whom I owe far more than I might ever be able to acknowledge and whose best quality was his inexhaustible gentleness, asked me to submit as a class assignment a "sequence." He was familiar with my passion for movies so he used the language of cinema to entice me. I could shape it as I wished, he said, but—herein the objective—it needed to be poetic. I didn't think I was interested in the challenge, so I told him poetry was too elusive for me. He asked me to give it a try.

I don't know what possessed me that night. I had taken public transportation that day to go buy some stamps. Or maybe I was on my way to art class. There was a park called Monumento Alvaro Obregón where I needed to catch my bus. I remember it well because it was a most gory place. Obregón, who was assassinated in late 1928, was a revolutionary hero known for nurturing his anticlerical sentiments. He was at an event in his honor at La Bombilla, a restaurant in the southern San Angel district—in the exact place where the monument was later built—when José de León Toral, a fervently religious cartoonist convinced that Obregón was the antichrist, approached him. He showed him his sketch pad. Obregón reached for it. Toral took out a pistol from his pocket, and pulled the trigger five times at close range. Obregón, a handsome man, died instantly.

In life he exemplified vengefulness. He had lost one of his arms—the right one, up to the elbow—during the revolution. Obregón recovered the arm and had it placed in a bottle of formaldehyde. A fine park was built where La Bombilla once stood and in it a museum-cum-monument for the arm. The bottled arm was located behind bulletproof glass. It was a gothic spectacle. While waiting for the bus

to come, I remember entering the monument and studying the arm carefully. Was it really Obregón's? Rumors had
it that a ransom was offered for anyone who recovered it
and the person who apparently found it is said to have
decimated a cadaver nearby and taken the arm, of roughly
Obregón's size, with him. Obregón was from the state of
Sonora. The story says that at least the owner of the actual
hand was also from there.

I remember reading all this in the information provided—was it on a plaque?—at the Monumento itself. The
place fascinated me. It was a house of horrors for sure but
there was something about it—the darkness of the main
gallery, the light that descended on the arm—that kept
me coming back twice, maybe thrice . . . and has kept the
image fresh in my mind. (By the way, I remember reading, around the same time, that when Napoleon died on
the island of Saint Helena, his penis—he was known to
have a notoriously minuscule one—was cut off and stolen.
For years reports of the whereabouts of Napoleon's penis
abounded in French society. Was it ever found? If so, in
what condition?)

In any case, approximately a block away from Monumento Alvaro Obregón, as the bus driver was speeding up,
a *campesina* woman unwisely crossed the street and found
herself in front of a yellow Volkswagen taxi. Its driver
couldn't brake in time and hit her. The woman went flying

up, made a pirouette in the air, and landed on the pavement with her legs split open. She appeared to be unconscious. I was on the bus and witnessed the accident from the window. The bus slowed down a bit, then continued on its course as if nothing extraordinary had taken place.

I was shocked. I came back home and told my mother the story. Later on I watched TV to see if a report had been filed but found nothing.

The next day I submitted a three-page scene about a funeral procession. It took place in San Angel, near the Monumento. I described the mourners in some detail. At the heart of the scene was a casket, which, surprisingly, didn't contain the corpse of the *campesina,* but that of José de León Toral, Obregón's assassin. Over his forehead a series of strange, illegible words were inscribed.

Days went by. I was nervous. Finally the teacher returned our papers. Mine came with a strong appreciative comment. He also suggested that I read the "sequence" out loud. I did and the students liked it as well. They described it as lyrical, even haunting. One of them said: "I can see it perfectly. I know what you're talking about! The death of poetry . . ."

Was that what I had intended to say? I don't think so. Honestly, I'm embarrassed by the assignment today. Was it about the death of the *campesina?* Or was it my intent to explore my sensations near Monumento Alvaro Obregón, a

place that made me experience uncomfortable thoughts—
and maybe even turned me into the spectator of gruesome
accidents—whenever I found myself near it?

Its contents are inconsequential, though. For what
happened on that day is that, unbeknownst to me, I was
hooked into literature. I came to realize that language, in
written form, had a tremendous power to invoke images. I
was able to make others *be* where I wanted them to be. And
I was able to make them think through images.

Yes, my composition was filled with spelling errors,
which the teacher underlined in blood red ink. But my
teacher saw something beyond my mistakes: he found a
story.

I was so proud I could barely convey my emotions to
my father. He was happy, in particular because Spanish
had never been a language I had felt close to. Yet the
teacher had made me feel more comfortable in it. In time
I would learn to see Spanish not as another tormenter but
as my ally, and later as a lover. In any case, that night I sat
down to write again. I set myself a task: Could I describe,
in cold terms, an inconsequential Coca-Cola can sitting
on my desk?

My objective was to produce a plotless portrait, to
present the can against its landscape, to refer to the rays of
sun on its surface, the shadow it projected on the wall. The
exercise didn't have a practical side to it: I wasn't going to

show it to my parents, teacher, or friends. I wanted to be the sole judge. I wanted the exercise to be an assessment of my linguistic skills: How elastic was my verbal bank? Did I have the talent to narrate the most mundane images around me through words?

I established a number of limitations: sentences needed to be short; all verbs needed to be in the present tense; and adjectives needed to be inserted in discreet, almost invisible fashion. Plus, I could not use a dictionary. I did place one next to me, though. I wanted it to be my witness. I told myself that once I had finished writing the description, I would plow through its pages in search of synonyms and antonyms. But only afterwards.

I still have the exercise I wrote that night stored somewhere in a drawer. I'm embarrassed by it now. But unlike the class assignment about the funeral procession, this one has a visible quality I'm proud of: *verve,* a word that has become my motto. It means vigor, dynamism. Literature doesn't describe the word, it redefines it.

> <

Verve—not long ago I came across this word in a crossword puzzle. It was serendipity, of course. For what else rules the universe if not sheer chance?

It wasn't I who was completing the puzzle. In fact, I dislike them. Or better, I'm terrible at them, a fact I find difficulty explaining given my logophilia. In any case, my mother-in-law, who opens the *New York Times Magazine* religiously every Sunday and completes the puzzle in about an hour, asked out loud: five-letter word, starting with *V*, meaning *vitality* but is not *vigor?*

Out of the blue, I gave her the correct answer. She looked at me with delight: "Hey, Ilan, your English is finally getting better!"

What she hadn't known—I didn't feel compelled to tell her—was that, by coincidence, *verve* was one of the words that stuck in my mind from playing *Fictionary.*

It simply stuck . . . and it pops up in my mind every so often, as a leitmotif of sorts.

My experience playing *Fictionary*—known in some circles as Balderdash—dates to that period. The rules are easy. A bunch of people gather together with a dictionary. Everyone is given small pieces of paper and a pencil. One of them looks for a peculiar word in the lexicon and reads it out loud but not its definition. I could say *verve* but let's try something else: *drosophila.* The assumption is that few will know its meaning. People then attempt to define the word in lexicographic language, e.g., as if it were defined in the dictionary. The reader also pencils down the actual definition. He then reads out loud, with equal seriousness, the available definitions. Herein four versions of *drosophila:*

1. A small fruit fly, used extensively in genetic research because of its large chromosomes, numerous varieties, and rapid rate of reproduction.

2. An evergreen eastern Asian shrub related to the tea plant, grown for its showy flowers and shiny leaves.

3. A strong, sweet liqueur made from a variety of bitter cherries.

And 4. a member of a group of indigenous people of South Africa and Namibia originally from the Drosophia region, traditionally nomadic hunter-gatherers. They belong to the larger Nama people and are the ancestors of the Griqua.

Who's right?

I remember playing *Fictionary* at evening parties. I was good at it. There was a captivating quality to the game, not only because of its social aspects (I love being *with* people), but because it indirectly pushed its players to engage in a succinct, almost telegraphic style.

I also remember coming home and, once daytime responsibilities were over, I would sit at my desk and imitate lexicographic entries by myself, just for the entertainment the exercise provided. It isn't viable because you're simultaneously the one copying the actual definition and the one concocting an alternative one. Still, it was thrilling to imagine different meanings of words. It was also attractive to learn to write with extreme clarity and brevity.

Eventually I wrote several more "sequences" for my middle-school teacher, each with some sort of allegorical twist. My spelling took years to improve. In Yiddish and Hebrew I had less trouble because I was called to write in these languages less frequently. But Spanish was a nightmare. In fact, I still made mistakes when, in my twenties, I was a correspondent in New York City sending dispatches across the Rio Grande to the newspapers *Excélsior* and *La Jornada*. At that point I was already becoming acquainted with English, a language I improved my skills in, only thanks to a case of chronic insomnia.

Anyway, as soon as I finished my first series of "sequences" in middle school, I started to read and read and read. . . . What prompted me to do it? I thirst to see how others managed to express the images in their minds. Stories were most endearing to me since they were also "sequences," e.g., mini-movies. Soon I understood that what interested me in literature wasn't only images but thought. A good story has a plot, but it also pushes us to think. Indeed, what is writing if not thinking?

Then and now, I let my envy go wild when I read. I stop and cherish an astonishing line, a paragraph, a page, and then wonder: Why can't I do the same? Literature is in the details. A fateful sentence can justify an entire life. So I look for that sentence as a reader. And I look for it as a writer. Yes, envy is a healthy sin. The dictionary offers some synonyms for it, *odium* and *opprobrium* among them. It defines *envy* as "the innermost desire to be someone else, or do what someone else does."

But . . . is this the right definition? How about "the attempt to do evil, harm and mischief as a result of a complex of inferiority"? Or else "the feeling of mortification and ill-will occasioned by the contemplation of superior advantages possessed by another"?

Yes, at some point I gave up my dream of becoming a filmmaker. I've forgotten when and where. I have no regrets.

It doesn't matter. I still like playing *Fictionary*. And I like reading definitions even more.

< 7 >

The Invention of Love

"Words make love with one another," André Breton said. But who invented love?

Animals don't know a thing about it: many mate and separate. Since language—verbal, that is—is a unique human quality, no other animal expresses affection and becomes neurotic about it.

Or do they? In my childhood, I had a dog, a cocker spaniel named Cookie—in Spanish, Cuki. She enjoyed sitting on my brother's bed as well as a mine for long hours, looking out the window at the passersby, airplanes, the sunset. She particularly enjoyed rainy afternoons, when a cloud of nostalgia descended on her. She would grow taciturn. Her gesture was contemplative, almost philosophical. What went on in Cuki's mind in such moments is impossible for me to know. She certainly was a love-starved pet.

In the neighborhood Cuki was known as a loner, enjoying the company of people but not of other dogs.

She lived with us for more than a decade. When my

siblings and I left home, Cuki also decided to change her life: one day after breakfast, she walked out the door and disappeared.

For weeks we looked for her in vain.

Approximately a year later, my parents moved to an apartment several miles away. One day they happened to drive by the old neighborhood and they spotted Cuki in a nearby park. They told me she was with a bunch of rowdy street dogs. My parents whistled. They called her name repeatedly. Cuki finally turned around. For a minute or two she looked at them with the same concentration she had when sitting on my bed. Then, in a pose of indifference, she looked at her fellow canines.

It took her less than a second to confirm the choice she had already made: Cuki rejoined her bunch.

She was never seen again.

Her love was significant, no doubt. But human love is different. Is it passion that makes a difference?

Passion is defined by the *OED* in a bizarre, almost mysterious fashion: "an eager outreaching of the mind . . . a vehement predilection." Of the mind, I say? Wasn't passion intimately rooted in the heart? And what does it mean to allow the mind to outreach, and to do so eagerly?

But back to *love:* the Acadians, Caldeans, Phoenicians, Sumerians, Babylonians, Egyptians, Normans, Toltecs, Vikings, and Quechuas didn't have a word for it, and hence didn't know a thing about it.

But we do . . . isn't that what matters? For love is a modern invention.

The word itself—*amóre* in Italian, *Любовь* in Cyrillic, *amour* in French, ﺣَﺐّ in Arabic, *amor* in Spanish, *liebe* in German, *love* in English—remind me of the definition Herbie Hancock gave for *jazz:* "It is something very hard to define but very easy to recognize." Go to your local drugstore and admire the greeting-card section: Hallmark Cards has made it its duty to define love a thousand different corny ways. Or pay attention—if you dare!—to Hollywood movies: from Clark Gable's "Frankly my dear, I don't give a damn!" to Ali McGraw's "Love means not ever having to say you're sorry," the possibilities are—for better or worse—infinite.

Love is abrasive, rowdy, obstinate, indomitable. Also, love is orderly, flexible, civilized. It is, in short, the sum of all contradictions and its negations as well. Can a lexicon encompass, in a single definition, such opposing thoughts? Can it say what it means and not simplify it at the same time?

Francesco Petrarca, in his *Life of Solitude* in the fourteenth century, might have been among the first to codify love and the correspondents Abelard and Eloise the first to experience it as ethos. But within Western Civilization (whatever the concept means, if it means anything at all), each culture defines love differently. To prove the point, I looked it up in a handful of translingual dictionaries, not in too many, in order to keep the scientific experiment within approachable boundaries.

First, of course, my *OED*. It takes the Oxford dons five pages and twelve columns to define it. "That disposition or state of feeling with regard to a person which (arising from recognition of attractive qualities, from instincts of natural relationship, or from sympathy) manifests itself in solicitude for the welfare of the object, and usually also in delight in his presence and desire for his approval." No sooner had I finished reading the definition than I remembered Dr. Johnson's *A Dictionary of the English Language*. He included the word *deosculation* to describe "the act of kissing." Only the lovable but love-conflicted British master would come up with such unromantic expression! Happily, oblivion has swept the term away. Otherwise, imagine a love scene in which Steve tells Arielle: "Let me deosculate you, for my heart burns in desire . . ."

The *Trésor de la langue française* is equally fertile in its definition, if also more ardent. *Amour,* it states, is the "*attirance, affective ou physique, qu'en raison d'une certaine affinité, un être éprouve pour un autre être, auquel il est uni ou qu'il cherche à s'unir par un lien généralement étroit.*" A loose translation: Draw, either physical or affective, that based on certain affinity, can be experienced toward another being, with whom one seeks to be united in a generally internal link. The French, as usual, bring in mystery to the art of love. There is an element of uncertainty, of plenitude in this definition. Then the erudite of the *Trésor* refers the reader to a 1937 novel by Jacques Chardonne, quoting its syrupy line *"L'amour, c'est beaucoup plus que l'amour."* No, love is sometimes more than just love, but also sometimes less.

I then went to María Moliner's *Diccionario del uso del español.* In its second edition, *amor* is described as *"sentimiento experimentado por una persona hacia otra, que se manifiesta en desear su compañía, alegrarse con lo que es bueno para ella y sufrir con lo que es malo."* An English interpretation: a feeling experienced by one person toward another, which manifests itself in the desire for company, in the happiness for what is good for that person and suffering for what is bad. Yes, the essence remains the same but the formulation is far less frigid than the *OED,* more warmhearted and—excuse the cliché—quixotic. The happiness for what is good and the suffering for what is bad? Ah, this is sheer melodrama.

Salvatore Battaglia's *Grande Dizionario della Lingua Italiana* includes pages and more pages in Italian on the word *amóre.* The definition states: *"Affetto intenso che tende al possesso del suo oggetto e all'unione con esso, e spinge a preservarne l'essere e procurarne il bene."* An attempt at translation: intense affection one possesses toward another object and its union with it, which requires its preservation and procures its well-being. The Italians appear to emphasize affection. They don't describe the entities experimenting love as human but simply as objects. Unlike Moliner, they don't talk about adversity: suffering? bad fate? No, love, in plain words, is the need for possession.

The *Deutsches Wörterbuch* by Brockhaus Wahrig announces this methodical definition for *Liebe: "tiefempfundene Zuneigung, starke gefühlsmäßige Bundung an einen anderen Menschen, verbunden mit der Bereitschaft, zu helfen. Opfer zu bringen, für den anderen zu sorgen usw."* An English version: deeply felt attraction toward another person, measured strongly through feelings of bonding together, which includes readiness to help, to sacrifice, and to worry about the other person's security. The Germans have not only described it more mathematically but also more religiously. The connection established by the definition is more spiritual: it includes sacrifice, bonding beyond the immediate, and the agony of wanting the other person safe and nearby.

Finally, I found this definition of *Любо́вь* in Cyrillic: "Чувство глубокои привязанности, преданности кому-, *чему-либо, основанное на признании высокого значени я, достоинства, на общих целях, интересах и т."* Again, an attempt at translation: a feeling of profound connection and dedication to someone or something that includes the sharing of interests. For the Russians love is a form of keenness and preservation, a sense of commonality that gives place to a partnership.

All this to say that the disparity between languages—and between cultures—is, invariably, a source of enjoyment. The attempt of foreign speakers to communicate with one another always results in humorous circumstances. Watch a Belgian engage in business with an Iranian while they communicate in English and you might witness some hairs being pulled off. Or observe a Peruvian and a Lithuanian in a classroom discussion of philosophical issues in German and you're likely to wonder if a couple of pints of Guinness wouldn't help to accomplish the task a bit faster.

This brings back the memory of when my wife Alison gave birth to Joshua. By then I had been in the United States more than half a decade. While I was proficient in English, its nuances often eluded me. Alison was my living dictionary, allowing me to grasp elusive meanings. These meanings would come only after hilarious exchanges.

One day, for instance, I heard the baby cry.

"He's angry," I said. "He needs to be fed . . ."

"Angry?" Alison answered. "Why would Josh be angry? He simply needs to be fed."

"Precisely. Since he's angry, he needs to eat."

"Did you do something to him, Ilan?"

"Me?"

"So why would he be angry?"

"Oh, please . . ."

"Do you mean upset?" she replied as she proceeded to give Josh a bottle.

"It's all the same."

"No, it isn't," Alison added.

"What's the difference?"

"Ilan, don't you know the difference between angry and upset?"

"I don't. Aren't they synonymous?"

Alison started laughing. She quickly sent me to the dictionary, where I discovered that *angry* means "passively affected by trouble," whereas *upset* is defined as, among other things, "a physical or (more commonly) mental disturbance or derangement." In other words, in one the action comes from the outside and in the other it is the product of internal change.

Why didn't I know how to distinguish between these terms? Easy: in Spanish the two are one and the same. I've seen Spanish/English-English/Spanish dictionaries differentiate them by establishing the former as *enfadado* and the latter as *trastornado*. But speakers—in Mexico, at least—use one instead of the other and vice versa. How could I have known that among Anglo-Protestants one needs to reckon with as many shades of baby emotion?

Needless to say, the issue is far more sophisticated when it comes to adult love. The traffic of affection between two individuals is challenging enough in any language. It can only become more taxing when the lovers don't speak the same tongue—and have no interpreter. Cervantes states in "The Dogs' Colloquy," part of his *Exemplary Novels,* that "it is as easy to say something stupid in Latin as it is in the vernacular." But it isn't a matter of recognizing that every language allows ample room for foolishness . . . and love, too. Love and foolishness are universal. Rather, the question is: Is love in one place the same as love in another?

Oftentimes, the best way to find a definition in a dictionary is to simply look up the wrong word. Years ago I read the best definition for *love.* I found it on a Hallmark card: "Love is a maelstrom." I looked up *maelstrom* in the *OED:* "a famous whirlpool in the Arctic Ocean on the west coast of Norway, formerly supposed to suck in and destroy all vessels within a long radius."

< 8 >

The Zebra and the Swear Word

In *Gulliver's Travels,* the protagonist journeys to the land of Houyhnhnms, where he discovers that in the kingdom there is no word to express lying or falsehood.

Think about it: What if we lived in a world without lies? Oh, but it would be so incredibly uninteresting.

(I should say that it isn't the case that among the Houyhnhnms lying is impossible. What Jonathan Swift simply means is that there is no such concept to define the activity itself in their society. An important difference, isn't it?)

Do dictionaries lie? Mark Twain once said: "One of the most striking differences between a cat and a lie is that a cat has only nine lives." What is the difference between a lie and an error? How about definitions shaped with tergiversation?

It takes some browsing to find out.

I'll concentrate on animals for now. This theme is as good as any to ruminate on lexicons "going over the edge," so to speak, without the browser necesssarily ever noticing it. You'd be amused by the portraits of them one is able to find in lexicons. Some of these portraits are veritable models of mathematical precision. A *cow,* for instance, is "the female of any bovine animal (as the ox, bison, or buffalo); most commonly applied to the female of the domestic species *(Bos Taurus)*."

Other animal definitions are laboriously scientific. A *pig (Porcus)* is described as "a South African quadruped *(Orycteropus capensis Cuv.)* about the size of a badger, belonging to the insectivorous division of the Edentata, where it occupies an intermediate position between the Armadillos and Ant-eaters."

For some reason, the makers of dictionaries seem always to be interested in animal skin. And, at least as far as the *OED* is concerned, lexicographers frequently like to find them in Africa. This isn't a surprise, given British colonial history. What is intriguing, though, is that the adjective *African* did not originally appear in the *OED.* Its preface explains why:

> the word *African* was one of the earliest instances in
> which the question of admission or exclusion arose
> with regard to an important adjective derived from a
> geographical proper name. After much careful consid-
> eration, and consultation with advisers, it was decided
> (perhaps by a too rigid application of first principles)

to omit the word, as having really no more claims to inclusion than *Algerian, Austrian* or *Bulgarian.* But when *American* was reached, some months afterwards, it was seen that *Americanize* and *Americanism* must of necessity be included, and that those ("with the *Americanizing* of our institutions") could not be explained without treating *American,* and explaining its restricted application to the United States. *American* was accordingly admitted. Then the question arose, whether the exclusion of African was consistent with the inclusion of *American;* but the question came too late; *African* had been actually omitted, on its own merits.

Anyway, back to animals. Quick: What's a *giraffe?* "A ruminant quadruped found in Africa," argues the *OED,* "remarkable for the length of its neck and legs, and for having its skin spotted like that of a panther."

Florid language, but no ambiguities here.

The one animal definition I find perplexing is the definition for *zebra:* "a South African equine quadruped (*Equus* or *Hippotigris zebra*), of whitish ground-colour striped all over with regular bars of black, inhabiting mountainous regions, and noted for its wildness and swiftness." Clearly, the lexicographer in charge of such a portrait has taken a leap of faith. Are zebras really white with black stripes? Or are they black with white stripes? Is the embrace of one of these approaches at the expense of the other a "tipping" of reality? Is there racism lurking in the lexicographer's background? Does the approach constitute a mere partiality or is it an error of judgment?

In the original of Guillermo Cabrera Infante's novel on nightlife in Cuba before Fidel Castro's revolution, *Three Trapped Tigers* (the book is also a rewriting of *Tristram Shandy*, by the way), there's a reference to the hilarious definition of *perro,* dog, in the *Diccionario de la lengua española* of the Real Academia. *"Mamífero doméstico de la familia de los cánidos, de tamaño, forma y pelaje muy diversos, según las razas, pero siempre con la cola de menor longitud que las patas posteriores, una de las cuales levanta el macho para orinar."* Herein an inevitably partial translation: domestic mammal of the canine family, coming in the most varied shape, form and fur, depending on its race, but always with a tail of shorter longitude than the hind legs, one of which the male raises to urinate. Needless to say, the definition brought the Academy such ridicule that the reference to male dogs raising their back leg to urinate has happily been eliminated, even though, you'll notice, real male dogs refuse to give up the habit.

Beyond the topic of animals but still tergiversation, in 1982, Gabriel García Márquez wrote a provocative essay on dictionaries. In it he pokes fun at another mistake, this one included in the legendary lexicon of María Moliner, a Spanish housewife who in 1967 decided, out of boredom, to compile, in her own handwriting, a lexicon of usage. García Márquez describes Moliner's volume, *Diccionario del uso del español,* as "the most complete, useful, abundant and entertaining in the Spanish language. It has two volumes and a total of 3,000 pages that weigh three kilograms, which makes it, consequently, more than twice the size of the dictionary of the Royal Academy of the Spanish Language and—in my judgment—more than twice as good." Amazing as it is in scope and quality, though, it isn't beyond embarrassments—no lexicon ever is. The word *día,* day, is described as the *"Espacio de tiempo que tarda el Sol en dar una vuelta completa alrededor de la Tierra."* Again, my translation: the space of time needed by the Sun to completely round the Earth. Did anyone ever wonder about the long-term impact the Inquisition had on Spain and its colonies? Well, the answer is as clear as the sun in the sky (and don't tell it to poor Galileo Galilei!). But García Márquez also derides the first portion of the definition: *the space of time.* Should such an erudite lexicon make a mistake of this type? Even though the expression is common in countless languages, it must either be space or time. It just can't be both! Apparently (and since plagiarism is a common practice among lexicographers), the error originates, again, in the lexicon of the Real Academia Española, where *day* is defined thus: *"tiempo que el Sol emplea en dar, aparentemente, una vuelta a la Tierra."* In English: the time the Sun takes to apparently circle the Earth.

Is an excess a tergiversation? Is it a lie? Dr. Johnson is guilty of a small number of excesses—"self-indulgences," perhaps—some of which are deliberate. He defined *oats* as "a grain which in England is generally given to horses, but in Scotland supports the people." He stated that *excise* is "a hateful tax levied upon commodities, and adjudged not by the common judges of property, but wretches hired by those to whom excise is paid." Lexicographer he famously portrayed as "a writer of dictionaries, a harmless drudge, that busies himself in tracing the original, and detailing the signification of words." *Essay* for him was "a loose sally of the mind; an irregular indigested piece; not a regular and orderly composition." Or take the word *internecine,* whose definition is recounted in Boswell's *Life of Johnson.* It means "deadly, destructive, characterized by great slaughter." But Johnson defines it as "endeavoring mutual destruction." That mutuality was injected by Johnson, and because of his authority, the definition stood accepted until the twentieth century, when the *OED* amended it.

An established rule in lexicography prohibits a definition to have a word simultaneously more difficult and more unrecognizable than the word defined. But Johnson broke the rule time and again. This is how, gloriously, he defined the word *network:* "any thing reticulated, or decussated, at equal distances, with interstices between the intersections."

What, in all honesty, constitutes a lie? In *Don Juan*, Canto II, Lord Byron writes:

> And, after all, what is a lie? 'Tis but
> The truth in masquerade.

The truth, when told with aggressive intent, can be more hurtful than a lie. And what is the difference between a mistake and a lie? Is there a difference between "lying innocently," as one of my middle-school teachers used to say, "and lying with malicious intent"?

Lies are the *sine qua non* of politicians. Ambrose Bierce defined *diplomacy* as "the patriotic art of lying for one's country." Politicians master the art of falsehood: they tell people what people are eager to hear. We have plenty of those around today, for sure. The relationship between language and thought is a thorny one in them. George Orwell once said: "If thought corrupts language, language can also corrupt thought."

The *OED* has an unusually short section for *lying*: "the action of telling lies." Curiously, the section on the other type of lying—"that which lies or rests in a recumbent, extended, stationary or inert position"—is somewhat longer.

Is this deliberate? In moral terms, lying is falsifying, being deceitful, and getting one's way by all means including the twisting of information. Can't the dictionary put it in those blunt terms?

Maybe because it enjoys twisting, wrapping, and reformulating. "Always speak the truth," says the Red Queen in *Through the Looking Glass,* "think before you speak, and write it down afterwards." The Red Queen tells this to Alice, not to the Cheshire Cat, whose smile is the epitome of sarcasm. And sarcasm, even when hidden, is found in any and all dictionaries. The erudites of the *OED* define it succinctly: "a sharp, bitter or cutting expression or remark." *Cat,* on the other hand, takes up about two three-column pages. At first, it is described, simply, as "the animal." Then, the *OED* goes into detail: "a well-known carnivorous quadruped *(Felis domesticus)* which has long been domesticated, being kept to destroy mice, and as a house pet." Happily, Lewis Carroll's cat refutes, at least in part, the Oxford don. For is there better proof of lack of domestication than a tendency to be sarcastic?

> <

Lexicographers not only tergiversate, but they are also fond of excluding what they dislike.

Take the word *fuck.* It is thanks to the American etymologist Allen Walker Read, best known for his studies into this term—part of a list of scatology, erotic behavior, and low-life opprobrium that has give headaches to generations of etymologists—that the word has been somewhat rehabilitated. (Read also dissected the term *okay*, as is seen in the tangential tribute paid to his contribution in Mencken's *The American Language*.) And it was because of R.W. Burchfield, chief editor of the *OED* from 1971 to 1984, that so-called "offensive parlance" officially entered the radar of the Oxford dons. Expressions like "Jew down" and "street Arab" also made it to the dictionary, as did, euphemistically, the "two key taboo words [which] start with letters towards the beginning of the alphabet."

At any rate, *fuck* is nowhere to be found in my 1971 edition of the *OED*. On page 1090 I'm able to locate *fucate* ("artificially coloured"), *fucation* ("the action of painting the face"), *fuchsite* ("a variety of muscovite containing chromium, which gives it a green colour"), *fuco'd* ("beautified with focus"), and *fucoid* ("resembling or belonging to seaweeds"). But, astonishingly, not *fuck*. And neither *fucking* nor *fucked*.

To use an idiom: Why the fuck isn't it there?

Thousands and thousands of words are recorded in the *OED* that no one uses right now. But fuck, arguably the most widely used one in the English-speaking world, or at least one of the most recurrent, is absent, ignored, obliterated.

Come on, Oxford dons, what's the moder-for-you?

They've noticed the concealment, for sure. They are even embarrassed by it. In *The New Oxford American Dictionary*—how new is it? well, it was published in 2001—they try to make amends. (By the way, the copy I have was given to me as a present by my mother-in-law. It includes this dedication: "For Ilan, Hanukkah 2001. Here are some more borrowed words!") On page 682, in a rectangular side bar, it states:

> Despite the wideness and proliferation of its use in many sections of society, the word *fuck* remains (and has been for centuries) one of the most taboo words in English. Until relatively recently, it rarely appeared in print; even today, there are a number of euphemistic ways of referring to it in speech and writing, e.g., the *F-word, f****, or *f—k*.

One cannot but be stunned (but not stoned!) by the durability and mutations of the word. A minuscule number of words in the English language are as flexible. I would even add that each tongue has its equivalent. The one I'm fond of is in Spanish, *chingar*, which Octavio Paz reflected on in *The Labyrinth of Solitude*, first published in 1950.

Excluding taboo words and other obscenities is an ancient lexicographic practice. Dr. Johnson himself was accused of such censorship. He was even confronted once by a lady and asked why his dictionary left them out. Johnson replied: "Madam, I hope I have not daubed my fingers. I find, however, that you have been looking for them."

Not only are lexicographers guilty by complicity, so are literati. Do Shakespeare's characters swear? They surely have inspired comments about them, though. In *Henry VI,* Part 2, Act III, Scene ii, Suffolk says:

> Would curses kill, as doth the mandrake's groan.
> I would invent as bitter-searching terms,
> As curst, as harsh, and horrible to hear,
> Deliver'd strongly through my fixed teeth,
> With full as many signs of deadly hate,
> As lean-faced envy in her loathsome cave:
> My tongue should stumble in mine earnest words;

Silence and exclusion . . . Edward Gibbon, in his book *The Decline and Fall of the Roman Empire,* mistakenly states, not without perplexity, that there isn't a single camel in the *Al-Qur'ān.* How is it that in such a quintessentially Arabic narrative the quintessential Arabic animal—oddly described by the *OED* as "a large hornless ruminant quadruped, distinguished by its humped back, long neck, and cushioned feet; it is nowhere found wild, but is domesticated in Western Asia and Northern Africa, in the arid regions of which it is the chief beast of burden" and by more preposterous describers as "a horse designed by committee"—is impossible to find? But in Gibbon's own ambitious autobiography, *Memoirs of My Life and Writing*, published in 1796, where he hopes to encompass everything he said and heard, not a single bad word appears. Was his life free of them? Had they been vanished like camels in the Al-Qur'ān?

The *Dictionnaire de l'académie française* made every effort to leave curse words out, and by doing so, established a pattern in French lexicography. But the citizens of the *République* have not eliminated them. In fact, some argue that there is a higher propensity in France today to use offensive speech than in the past. It may all be just an impression, but there is little doubt that if the *Dictionnaire* didn't preserve these delicacies, its users surely did. Johnson also purged the British language of his time from irreverence and Sir James Murray, who was a devout Christian, seconded him. Noah Wesbster didn't want much to do with this aspect of language. Did they all "do the right thing"? Of course not. They were dwellers of their own prudish age, but it is a shame that, in attempting to record the geographical vastness of English, they left out what was most immediate to them: the ugly yet enchanting side of parlance.

The definition in *The New Oxford American Dictionary* is succinct: "1., to have sexual intercourse with someone; and 2., to ruin or damage something." But the syntactical incarnations are manifold. *Fuck* is used as a verb ("Antonio fucks Néstor's sister"), a noun ("The problem's a fuck"), an adjective ("The hotel is fucking beautiful"), and as an adverb ("Antonio fucking knows how to manipulate"). A person might be *fucker* and a *fuckwit,* and also be *fucked up.* And one might *fuck around* and *fuck up* until one will be asked to *fuck off.* Or else, a female might be sexually inviting by saying, *fuck me.* Plus, there are expressions such as *Don't fuck with me!* and *Go fuck yourself!*

Jonathan Green, a lexicomaniac like myself, once pointed out that "the most absurd example of such squeamishness is the absence of the resolutely standard English term *sexual intercourse* from virtually all American college dictionaries." Everybody does it! Everybody uses the word to describe it! So why the pedantry?

Happily, more recent editions of the *OED* have opened up, finally: *motherfucker* and *cocksucker* are in it now, safeguarded for the ages. Will the fact that these obscenities are no longer outside the realm of dictionaries make them less attractive to people? After all, the allure of the forbidden is disappearing.

Or is it? *Fuck* is part of the large reservoir of words often described as cacophonies. *Cacophony* is "the use of harsh-sounding words" and *cacology* is a "bad choice of words. " But my favorite word in this category is *cacography,* defined by the dictionary, in part, as "the science of bad handwriting." (Should the definition be upgraded to "the science of bad calligraphy"?) The Latinate root of the prefix is *caco* = bad. According to my mother, the first word I ever uttered was *caca*—or imitating her imitating me: *ca-ca*—which in most Romance languages means shit.

Lexicons used to be notorious for avoiding swear words. And up until World War II, writers in general took a similar approach. Ambrose Bierce defined *euphemism* thus in *The Devil's Dictionary*: "a figure of speech in which the speaker or writer makes his expression a good deal softer than the facts would warrant him in doing." And Woody Allen tells the following joke: "Some guy hit my fender the other day, and I said onto him, 'Be fruitful and multiply.' But not in those words."

Yet cacophony has always been incredibly alluring, even when it was most prohibited. Probably no words in the lexicon are in more demand, and acquire as many meanings, as the so-called "list of forbidden terms," so forbidden that everyone uses the words all the time. Last summer, my oldest son Joshua and I decided to conduct an experiment. He would take pencil and pad with him to his camp in Chicago and would record as many swear words as he could in the three-week period, which was the overall length of his retreat. Before he left we made a bet: Josh estimated eighteen different terms, I predicted thirty-eight. I was closer to target. The miscellaneous list goes like this:

> ass
> asshole
> balls
> bastard
> bitch
> bonehead
> boobs
> bull
> bullshit
> butt
> Christ
> *carbón*
> *coño*
> crap
> cunt
> damn
> dick
> dickhead
> dickless
> dork
> dumb
> fag

fuck

geek

goddamn

gosh

heck

hell

Holyshit

idiot

Jesus

jerk

motherfucker

moron

pendejo

penishead

pinche

pissed off

scumbag

scumface

shit

shithead

son-of-a-bitch

stink

stupid

sucker

wacking off

whore

Grand total: forty-eight.

Choose your favorite! Or better, choose them all!

The children at the camp were between twelve and seventeen years of age. Josh said males swore far more frequently than females. But is this true in general?

There are all sorts of swearing, among them, profanities, vulgarities, obscenities, insults, slurs, and scatological references. Sexual organs, in particular, are a magnet today. Is it true that there are 1,300 different words for *dick?* And is that number larger than the synonyms for *boobs?*

The use of cacophonies is a form of merriment. Does it minimize the moral standing of the speaker? Maybe in the olden days but not anymore: people use them constantly—even America's vice president. Ecclesiastes' argument that there is a time and place for everything under the sun doesn't apply to these words. Are they better used outside the classroom and office, far from one's parents and other authorities, only among a small, discreet circle of friends? Well, yes, but they seldom stay there.

Or do they?

Swear words are loud. They are also popular. And why shouldn't they be? That which is banned is most delicious. Mark Twain was right: "Let us swear while we may, for in heaven it will not be allowed."

< 9 >

Gladys

I've known Ramona Gladys Pérez Lozano for years—how many exactly, I forget. I value her friendship dearly. Her story is at once common and perplexing, with an unfortunate dose of disaster.

Gladys is from El Salvador. She came to the United States in 1996 as an undocumented laborer, not speaking a word of English. She was thirty years old at the time. Her mother had died giving birth to her thirteenth child. The father got frightened right away. How would he take care of more than a dozen children, none of them yet fifteen? He had a propensity for alcohol. He would disappear late in the afternoon and would not come back until next morning. In one of his escapades, he disappeared for good. The kids were as good as orphans.

The poor are sometimes able to look fate in the eye and recognize in themselves exceptional strategies of survival: they don't easily give in to depression ("the action of lowering, or process of sinking"). Gladys's oldest siblings took charge. Everyone who was capable of it got a job. Gladys was

nine years old at the time. She quit school. She never completed first grade. She is still barely able to read and write.
When she sends me a note, it is in preteen handwriting.

In time Gladys herself gave birth to three kids: Oscar,
Fanny, and Elizabeth. She never married her children's
father. They lived together for a couple of years. Then he,
too, disappeared.

Two of Gladys's siblings left El Salvador for Massachusetts. They each took three weeks to make the move.
The United States–Mexico border is notoriously harsh. But
their trouble began in the border between Guatemala and
Mexico. The Mexican border patrol caught them and beat
them. A *coyote*—from the Nahuatl *coyotl,* traditionally
understood as a carnivorous, canine animal smaller than
the wolf, but in this usage a smuggler of undocumented
immigrants into the United States—was helping Gladys's
siblings. They promised him $1,500. Part of the deal was
that they would attempt the crossover three times. After
that, they would be on their own. Fortunately, they crossed
the Guatemala–Mexico border on the third try. They successfully crossed the United States–Mexico border on their
second attempt.

Years later, already settled down—one worked at La
Veracruzana, a small-town ethnic restaurant owned by
a former gang member from Los Angeles, the other at a
Howard Johnson's—they sent for Gladys. It took her thirty-

six days to make the transnational journey. She walked, took rides, hid in trains and trucks, and ate thanks to the mercy of strangers. She assured me she spent the equivalent of $65 overall. She finally made it to the outermost point of Mexico. In the dead of night, she shrank under a fence, at the coyote's instructions, and desperately ran for almost a mile across a desert. Gladys heard gunshots behind her, but didn't look back. Someone was waiting for her in a blue Chevrolet. They drove her to Douglas, Arizona. A couple of days later she was taken to Phoenix. From there she took a flight to Hartford. She had never been on an airplane in her entire life. As the plane took off, she peed in her pants.

Gladys lived at first in her sibling's one-bedroom apartment. A total of eight Salvadorans lived there, six male and two female. She worked in a pizza parlor, a hair salon; she cleaned people's houses, swept floors at a Holiday Inn, and worked as a dishwasher in an Italian restaurant called Pinocchio's. It was around then that I met her.

Before going to work, I used to stop at a café called Rao's that sells strong, freshly brewed Colombian coffee. It's the type of place where artists, students, and misfits hang out—not your typical immigrant parlor. But it was on Gladys's way to the bus station, so she often stopped to get an espresso to go. I would hear her communicate with the person behind the counter. Gladys would use a maximum of three words: "espresso, please" and *"tenkyu."*

I exchanged a smile with her and then, the next day, I said something in Spanish. Her eyes sparkled. She was relieved to hear someone use her native tongue. She immediately became talkative. Gladys told me where she was from, the number of hours she worked cleaning houses, and so on.

The next time we saw each other she told me more. I also told her about my own upbringing, my two kids, and about my students.

We became friends.

She also worked for a while at La Veracruzana. I would go for breakfast there every so often with my friend Martín. Gladys would prepare delicious *huevos rancheros* and *chilaquiles* for us. If the clientele wasn't too demanding, she would come sit for a few minutes at our table.

Eventually I convinced Gladys, after some months, to attend English lessons. I found a place conveniently located—the second floor of the Fleet Bank—where free classes were offered to immigrants. I once went to visit a class. The majority of the students were from China and Malaysia. I also saw some Haitians. I was surprised not to see more Latinos—only three or four in a classroom of roughly fifteen students.

Gladys began to go every Wednesday. But she had a terribly rough time. "Ay, Ilan, *no puedo pronunciar las palabras,*" she would tell me in a Salvadoran-accented Spanish.

Pronouncing the most basic English words was excruciatingly difficult for her. "The teacher says I need to study harder. But I don't have time. . . . Last time I was in school I was a *chipota*. My mother, before she died, told me always to go to school. But I haven't been able to. It's hard!"

I help Gladys as much as possible. We repeat words together and we go over her spellings. *Gur morne, ticher. Ai am fain. An jau ar yu?*

> <

Whenever I see Gladys, I think of my own odyssey as an immigrant across the Rio Grande. But lately I've been reflecting less at a personal level. I have been compelled to see the broader canvas before me. How do immigrants become Americans? By what innate, unfathomable metamorphosis do we cease being the people we were upon arrival and go about acquiring altogether new selves?

I am particularly attracted to the subject from the perspective of language. America has always benefited from languages other than English. Since the first polyglot encounter between Pocahontas and John Smith, the Puritans and Indians in the sixteenth century figured out ways to interpret—to translate, to reinvent—one another. The miraculous aspect of the endeavor, though, is that no matter what the circumstances were, the English language always prevailed. It was, is now, and is likely to remain the great, undefeated equalizer. This is, needless to say, a good thing: for the nation to remain one, homogeneous yet pluralistic, the mastering of the vernacular is the only viable step in the process of assimilation. *Parlez-vous anglais? Mai oui.* Okay, so please join the party.

Gladys's journey is not unlike that of millions before her. They arrived speaking Swahili, Creole, Cantonese, Italian, Yiddish, Portuguese . . . and, years later, they, or more often their children and grandchildren, have left the immigrant parlance behind.

Is the situation changing? In the small Massachusetts town where Gladys lives there are barely enough Latinos to make a soccer match happen. But that isn't the case in the rest of the nation. Plus, the number of Asians is also growing rapidly. These waves of newcomers are learning English at a rapid speed. And yet, they—I'll change the pronoun now: *we*—are arriving in such gargantuan numbers that the capacity to assimilate, to become American in the traditional sense, is being subverted. Spanish for sure has become the country's unofficial second language. To handle yourself well in numerous parts of the United States today, you need Cervantes's tongue as much as you need Shakespeare's.

The desire to incorporate others into the so-called Melting Pot results in impatience toward non-English speakers. Billy Wilder said: "I don't object to foreigners speaking a foreign language; I just wish they'd all speak the same foreign language." Increasingly for the gringos any interest in the rest of globe has been reduced to a condescending attitude best represented by my good ol' Uncle Stanley of Long Island. Once, after he congratulated me for having learned the English language, I said: "It's now your turn, *Tío Estanli*. You have to learn Spanish now." His was a laconic response: "But why should I, Ilan, when you can already talk with me rather nicely?"

My initial reaction to attitudes like Uncle Stanley's is always one of pity. *Tío Estanli* is clearly all the poorer for his monolingualism. Or is he? Then I remember that he himself is a child of Jewish immigrants from Poland. When he was a child Stanley spoke English in the street and at school. His parents also made every effort to use English at home, although their English was half baked and they made mistakes. Yiddish was heard in the household when the parents didn't want the kids to understand something. It became a forbidden language.

Years later, it remains forbidden, not only Yiddish but any other foreign tongue. A well-known joke asks: How does one refer to a person who speaks four languages? Tetralingual. A person who speaks three languages? Trilingual. Two? Bilingual? And only one language? An American.

America is an international power but, curiously, it is a culture allergic to foreignness.

In fact, my dialogues with *Tío Estanli* once led us to a fascinating *Via Crucis.* So much distress goes into another language. If English is the *lingua franca* of the twenty-first century, why not turn it—officially, that is—into a *lingua universalis?* Why, in his own words, "doesn't everyone in the world just come to their senses and switch to American English? Can you imagine the amount of business and diplomatic hurdles that would solve?"

I pretended to be gung ho about it. "Yeah, yeah, it's a brilliant idea . . . !" The end of communication that often leads to warfare, the end of disparity that frequently results in famine.

Okay, so my uncle's suggestion isn't altogether new. The objective he's after is a sensitive one whose roots go back to . . . well, think about it: Isn't the Tower of Babel to be blamed for all the confusion around?

Before Babel, we are told, there was a universal language. Then humankind became conceited and tempted the Almighty. In return, G-d sent us as punishment the multiplicity of languages that has defined human endeavors ever since. Babel points to a simpler, purer origin. The resulting trauma is the initiation of a period of verbal plentitude. Today we live in a world with some 5,000 different tongues.

To me that plurality is exquisite. But not to *Tío Estanli.* So, as he puts it, why can't we return to the origin?

The attempt to return to a pre-Babelic period is deeply rooted in history. People have defined Hebrew (and at times, Latin, too) as a primal language. Also, people have sought to find a universal tongue capable of abolishing all others. In the nineteenth century, an age known for its romanticism, the desire acquired the form of several ur-languages, including Esperanto. The product of the Polish linguist Dr. L. L. Zamenhof, Esperanto was established mathematically in 1887 after years of research. Zamenhof proposed it was a second language that would allow people who speak different native tongues to communicate. This meant that no linguistic and cultural identity would be under threat, but a common verbal code would be established to bring an end to violence. Esperanto, it is said, is four times easier to learn than other languages.

Earlier in time, efforts to codify a universal language entertained European thinkers, among them Francis Bacon, René Descartes, Athanasius Kircher, and Gottfried Wilhelm Leibniz. Another one of them, arguably the most intellectually sophisticated, was John Wilkins, a seventeenth-century Briton who was a member of the Royal Society and the author of, among other books, *An Essay Towards a Real Character and a Philosophical Language,* published in 1668. The premise is straightforward: there is a universal grammar and a universal lexicon with which a universal phonology can be connected. The yearning to see reason as the ultimate unifier is a product of the Encyclopedic age and it has a religious background. Before the building of the Tower of Babel, in what language did people—Adam and Eve, Cain and Abel, Noah and his wife, et al—communicate? The answer is the pristine, original (e.g., universal) language of Paradise, the one G-d used to make himself understood to his progeny.

Four years before his *Essay,* Wilkins wrote:

> As men do generally agree in the same Principle of Reason, so they do likewise agree in the same Internal Notion or Appreciation of things. That external Expression of Mental notions, whereby men communicate their thoughts to one another, is either to the Ear, or to the Eye. . . . So that if men should generally consent upon the same way or manner of Expression, as they do agree in the same Notion, we should then be freed from that Curse in the Confusion of Tongues, with all the unhappy consequences of it.

Wilkins suggested a relatively easy linguistic system. He organized words according to categories (which he also called classes). These categories were in turn divided into differences, and the differences were divided into species. Borges, in one of his sleepless nights, made a chart of Wilkins's approach. "He assigned to each class a mono-syllable of two letters; to each difference, a consonant; to each species, a vowel. For example, *de* means element; *deb,* the first of the elements, fire; *deba;* a part of the element fire, a flame." Borges praised the system.

> Let us consider the eighth category: the category of stones. Wilkins divides them into common (flint, gravel, schist), modics (marble, amber, coral), precious (pearl, opal), transparent (amethyst, sapphire), and insolubles (coal, chalk, and arsenic). Almost as surprising as the eighth is the ninth category. This one reveals to us that metals can be imperfect (cinnabar, mercury), artificial (bronze, brass), recremental (filings, rust), and natural (gold, tin, copper). Beauty belongs to the sixteenth category: it is a living brood fish, an oblong one.

It makes sense, except that language . . . well, language doesn't always make sense. What about ambiguities? What about redundancies? One single aspect of language messes up the whole approach: *usage.* People first learn to use a word and then they adapt it to their circumstances. Could language be structured logically? It surely could, but it wouldn't make it too practical. Jacques Barzun of Columbia University once said that

usage is not an agent but a result—the result of in-
numerable "votes" cast over the years for or against
a particular word. The leaders in this popular choice
are the men who write and speak professionally—the
Roosevelts and Churchills, Hemingways and Audens.
If, as often happens, such a man is also a theorist about
his own art, he will tell us his loves and his hates among
vocables. As user and critic, he himself is the voice of
usage, himself his own highest authority, with power of
life and death over any current form. And as old words
are not sacred and may be changed, so new ones are not
sacred and may be liquidated. It is the one instance in
which rational killing is no murder.

Plus, usage is what makes art possible. Could Wilkins's
disciplined invention allow for the production of novels and plays? I doubt it. A language has to be malleable
enough to be able to communicate the complexities of its
age. And would a universal language that is shaped artificially, in the security of a laboratory, solve Gladys's problem? Not in the least.

And should *Tío Estanli* be turned into a prophet and
English be imposed on the rest of humankind?

History holds the answer.

> <

Gladys's urge to memorize the English vocabulary against all odds had made me think, time and again, of two books I read long ago. I cherish them enormously. They granted me a precious understanding of that most ethereal, evanescent human capacity: memory. (Flaubert, in his *Dictionnaire des idées reçues*, said of memory: "Complain of your own; indeed boast of not having any. But roar like a bull if anyone says you lack judgment.") The volumes were both written by a Russian neurologist, who was professor of psychology at the University of Moscow, Aleksandr Romanovich Luria. (I've seen an alternative transliteration from the Cyrillic: Luriia). One of them was *The Man with a Shattered World: The History of a Brain Wound*, about a soldier named Zasetsky who suffers a terrible injury in the battlefield in Smolensk in 1943 and loses his capacity to fully remember events as a result. He is able to recall his childhood but not his recent past. He also loses half of his field of vision. Plus, he has trouble writing, reading, and speaking. The other book is, in a way, a response to the first: *The Mind of a Mnemonist: A Little Book About a Vast Memory*, about a man—he is called S., a device, needless to say, reminiscent of Kafka—with a portentous memory, one of whose attributes is the incapacity to forget.

When I first switched to English in search of a literary language to better express myself, I wrote a long story set in the Czech Republic and Mexico and inspired by

Luria. It was called "The Invention of Memory." (It is part of *The One-Handed Pianist*.) Its protagonist, one Zdenek Stavchansky, a freak with an enviable talent to remember, is suddenly diagnosed with an illness that will erase his memory altogether. He chooses to travel to his mother's native home, Mexico, and attempt to re-create as frequently as possible, in the theater of his mind, the various episodes that constitute his life.

I also wrote an essay, "Memory and Literature," a meditation on books and remembrance. I'm not interested in rehashing the same ideas again. My interest has shifted to words. Doesn't the *OED* define *reason* single-mindedly as memory? What is the connection between words and memory? For one thing, it's clear that communication is impossible without the faculty to remember words at a precise time, and to fit those words into the mental train of thought. Brain-damaged patients, for instance, often have to relearn how to speak. They are taught how to slowly move their facial muscles again. But the effort often needs to go further. They need to retrieve words from their verbal reservoir. Is that reservoir still available? Have they forgotten it? If they have, the process will require becoming a child again, so to speak. They will be forced to enhance their memory banks by naming things one by one.

Gladys knows that a *tenedor* in Spanish is the word that

refers to "an instrument with two, three or four prongs, used for holding the food while it is being cut, for conveying it to the mouth, and for other purposes at table or in cooking." So the connection between object and sound has been established. Her objective is to move onward to the acquisition of *another* word for the exact same object: *tenedor, fork.*

When Gladys turned thirty-three, I gave her a bilingual dictionary for her birthday.

It was her idea. "The teacher showed us one. What is it?"

I told Gladys it's a list of words, with their respective meanings. The one she needed, I said, was a bilingual one. "You look up a word in Spanish and it will give you the English." In my office in the third floor of my home, I showed her a Spanish/English lexicon.

She had no clue. "Look! Words and more words," I explained. "Every single one you'll ever need."

I forgot about the incident. Time went by. When I recalled that her *cumpleaños* was around the corner and asked her what she wanted for a present, she replied: *"Un diccionario."*

I got one wrapped. Gladys was excited. She opened it right in front of me, looked at it, and then said she needed to go back to work.

"Wait!"

I told Gladys we could look up a word. "*¿A ver?* Is my name in it?"

"I'm afraid not," I replied. "This dictionary doesn't include names."

I waited to see her reaction. Gladys was disappointed. I felt somewhat awkward. I was trying to help my dear friend handle an instrument that is useful only when one is able to handle oneself freely in a language. In a way, it was like showing a Mapa Mundi to someone who has never left his birthplace and does not suspect there's life anywhere but there. (In fact, in Flaubert's story "A Simple Heart," a scene exactly like that occurs.)

Then I said: "You could look for the word *tenedor . . .*"

She smiled but felt a little ashamed, too. "*¿Cómo le hago,* Ilan?"

I shouldn't have been surprised by her response. A person with a limited education doesn't know what to do with a dictionary. He might understand what it is, but to use it he would need lots of practice. The mere idea that words are organized alphabetically is a challenge. Gladys, it became clear to me, knew the alphabet, but it is hard for her to go automatically to the letter *P.* She has to recite the alphabet in her memory a letter at a time, then browse through the lexicon pages. It's a considerable effort, to say the least.

The next day when I saw Gladys she said: "I don't know

why to use the dictionary you gave me. I already know the words in Spanish. Everybody does . . ."

"But you don't in English."

"*Sí,* I don't," I said. "But I can ask my teacher."

> <

Some eighteen months ago, Gladys paid a coyote $3,500 to bring her son Oscar from El Salvador to Massachusetts. The travel took him three weeks. He also works at Howard Johnson's now.

Oscar's language fascinates me even more. Unlike his mother, he graduated from high school in El Salvador, so the Spanish tools he arrived with in the United States were more helpful. Still, his English-language skills were primitive. Oscar could say *hello, good-bye, how much does it cost?, where is the restroom?,* and other similar expressions, but little in the way of complex conversation.

He began attending Gladys's classes and learned much faster than his mother. He also enrolled in a public technical school twice a week. It is in a town some twelve miles away. As a result Oscar began to socialize with other Latinos. His linguistic pattern, thus, has moved in directions different from Gladys's.

He mixes Spanish and English much more. This is an important aspect that recalls my conversations with *Tío Estanli.* Oscar is starting to speak in Spanglish, the mixture of English and Spanish. A jargon? Carl Sandburg described *slang* as the "language which takes off its coat, spits on its hands, and goes to work."

In the last decade or so, I've spent countless hours studying Spanglish. How does it evolve? Is it a recent verbal phenomenon? Are there precedents in the United States? Elsewhere in the globe, what are the similarities between Spanglish and say Franglais, Portuñol, Hebrabic, and Chinglish? Is Spanglish a dialect? And does it appear to be evolving syntactically in such a way that might lead to the formation of a full-fledged language? I even compiled a lexicon of some 6,000 of its terms.

Spanglish has a long and rich history. Its roots are traceable as far as back as the Guadalupe Hidalgo Treaty of 1848, when, after the Mexican-American War, two-thirds of the Mexican territory was sold to the United States for $15 million. Those territories were mostly inhabited by Spanish-speaking dwellers who abruptly found themselves exposed to English and an Anglo-Protestant way of life. In newspapers and legal documents of the period there are traces of Spanglish words and syntactical formulations.

Another time of intense linguistic experimentation occurred during the Spanish-American War of 1898, when Spain finally ceded its colonies in the Caribbean Basin. Cuba and Puerto Rico entered the orbit of influence of the United States, thus embarking—each of them in different fashion—in a cultural life in which English formed an integral part.

It is difficult to establish precisely how many people use Spanglish, as well as when and how often they use it every day. Unquestionably, it is used on a regular basis in Puerto Rico (population 2 million) and the United States–Mexico border (approximately added population: 25 million). But it is also heard in major urban centers such as Miami, New York, Los Angeles, San Antonio, Chicago, Dallas, Boston, and so on. You hear it used primarily in the home, the street, the community center, the classroom, and the office.

Studies have established that Spanglish speakers can be bilingual (English and Spanish) and also monolingual (either English or Spanish). They belong to different social strata: low-income workers, middle-class professionals, upper-class entrepreneurs, etc. This means that Spanglish is neither defined by class or by race or ethnicity. Latinos and other speakers of every background use it.

In my travels I've come to recognize three verbal strategies used by Spanglish speakers: [1] code-switching, e.g., the free-travel from English to Spanish and vice versa ("Yo went to la store"); [2] automatic and simultaneous translation (e.g., expressions like *"Te llamo pa'trás!"*); [3] and the coining of new terms (*marqueta* for market, *grincar* for green card, *rufo* for roof). Depending on where geographically and temporally Spanglish speakers might use it, the syntactical foundation is either English- or Spanish-based.

As more detailed scholarship accumulates, it is clear that there isn't one Spanglish but a whole variety. Each Latino national group has its own variety. Thus, there are Pocho, Pachuco, and Chicano forms of Spanglish; you can find Cubonics, Nuyorrican, Dominicanish, and so on. This is because the Spanish in Latin America isn't homogeneous: each country has its own distinct type (Ecuadorian Spanish, Peruvian Spanish, Venezuelan Spanish, etc.). As immigrants from the Hispanic world move to the United States, they bring with them their own national syntax and vocabulary, which in turn influences the way Spanglish evolves. But the multiplicity of Spanglish is also defined by location: Chicano Spanglish in El Paso, Texas, is different from Chicano Spanglish in Portland, Oregon.

The growth of Spanglish, I believe, is, to a large extent, the result of a number of factors: an unabated Hispanic immigration to the United States; the triumphs and pitfalls of Bilingual Education; the spread of multiculturalism as an ideology; and globalization as a cultural pattern at the beginning of the twenty-first century.

Yes, there are many other hybrid languages in the world: for example, Portuñol (a mix of Portuguese and

Spanish spoken in the border of Spain and Portugal as well as Brazil and countries like Venezuela) and Franglais (the cross between French and English, spoken on both sides of the English Channel, in the Caribbean and parts of Africa). But Spanglish is a far more complex verbal way of communication, mainly because, unlike other border dialects, it is surely used by a huge number of speakers (more than the total population of Spain or Argentina).

Some argue that Spanglish is but a middle step in the process of English-language acquisition. This means that as soon as Latinos abandon Spanish completely and become fully fluent in English, Spanglish will disappear. These specialists use as evidence the experience of previous immigrants to the United States. Among Jewish immigrants from Russia and Eastern Europe, for instance, Yiddish gave place to Yinglish, which in turn gave place to English. Roughly a century after the first Yiddish-speaking Jewish immigrants arrived to American shores, the vast majority of American Jews speak no Yiddish. A similar pattern was followed by Germans, Italians, and other immigrants.

This argument is flawed. Latinos immigration, for one thing, has been constant for over a century and doesn't show signs of diminishing. Plus, the closeness of the immigrant's old home (Mexico, Guatemala, Puerto Rico, the Dominican Republic . . .) and the relatively inexpensive travel fares make mobility back and forth relatively easy. This means Spanish doesn't disappear from the landscape like other immigrant languages have done.

Oscar's ordeal has allowed me to appreciate, in an immediate way, the use of Spanglish as a form of communication.

Once I saw Oscar at a baseball game where my son Josh was playing for the Reds in the Babe Ruth League. I was seated in the bleachers when Oscar showed up with other teenagers. He saw me and came to say hello. We talked for a few minutes. I mentioned that I was quite impressed by his use of English. "You're really learning it fast, my friend," I said. I also told him I was spellbound by the way he—like myself—sometimes intertwined words from both languages.

"A Gladys no le gusta," he said. "But she does it, too." And then Oscar asked, "Why is it wrong if what ya' sayin' is clear?"

Oscar is a sharp young man and that was a sharp question. Yes, why is it that the mixing of two perfectly circumscribed languages is forbidden? Why do people in Berlin take offense when German and Turkish are intertwined, immediately decrying impurity? Why don't the French like using English terms in their speech?

The image that crossed my mind as Oscar went back to his peers was of a dictionary like the *OED* that would include, in a major soup of backgrounds, words from scores of languages. Not a bilingual lexicon, not even a multilingual one, but one defined by chaos. Why not?

Why do we create barriers between tongues? How has it come to be that children are taught to speak and write in a particular language and not to borrow from another linguistic bank? American English is astoundingly elastic. Words from other tongues—called loan words—are always being incorporated into its verbal bank. Dozens, for instance, come from Algonquin dialects, including *moccasin, pecan, powwow, skunk, squash, totem,* and *wigwag.* Or else, think of more recent acquisitions from French, German, Italian, Spanish, etc., such as *divorcée, media, lasso, libretti, paparazzi, parfait, piñata, sauerkraut, soprano, taco,* and *virtuoso.*

I believe I have the answer: language is a ticket to identity. To mix languages is to appear confused. The Hungarians speak Hungarian, the Italians Italian, the Czechs Czech, and the Russians Russian. If and when a Russian introduces Chechen into his Russian speech, he is called a double agent, a conspirator, maybe even a defector. Language is infused with nationalism. Like the flag and the national anthem, it is the stuff that makes a nation unique. And uniqueness means rejection—or at the very least, separation—of other people's heritage.

And yet, languages have intermingled with one another since the moment the first Sumerian, Phoenician, and Babylonian merchants offered their goods to others: to interact is to let one's language be exposed to change, to enrich oneself through the speech of others. What is Early English if not the outcome of the jumbled parlance used by the Celts, the Romans, the Saxons, the Vikings, and the Normans? Isn't that part of the magic of the kennings in *Beowulf*? And how did Yiddish come to be if not by using German morphology and Hebrew characters? Didn't Spanish in the eleventh century evolve from vulgar Latin and the incipient dialects of the Iberian Peninsula? People lament the death of a language in Africa, South America, and India. But how about applauding the birth of cross-fertilized tongues? These are born in the modern world thanks to globalization, the exact same globalization that kills aboriginal speech.

It has been a difficult battle but interracial marriages are more a norm than ever before. Folklore, food, and culture are also juxtaposed. Might language follow the same road then? Will the intercourse of different tongues ultimately be accepted?

Oscar at times talks a mumbo jumbo like the one tourists use. That, too, is a consequence of his late-in-life northbound immigration and his socializing with other Latino kids. In fact, as I listen to him I wonder if anyone ever attempted a dictionary of "immigrant-speak"? On the other hand, there is also the jargon improvised by tourists as they struggle to communicate in countries whose language they hardly speak. A dictionary of *tourisms?* By this I don't mean a lexicon that tells a traveler how to say the simplest expressions—"Where's my change?" and "Is there a lavatory?" Instead, I'm referring to the way tourists think they know how to utter these expressions in Swahili and Tagalong. I don't know if there's a bundle to be made there, but at the very least, there is a possibility for plenty of laughter.

In an e-mail exchange with a student of mine who lives in Japan, I told her about Oscar and about my interest in tourisms. She immediately sent me back, in an attachment, a compendium of what she called "gems of Japanized English." It included the following sentence found near an out-of-service elevator at Narita Airport: "An escalator avobe this notice is under repair hopeing to be savoured with yours use of northern escalator or elevator." The attachment also had this line, which, according to my student, first appeared at Expo '70: "WARNING Gentlemen! Please do not carry your wallets in rear pocket for your backside is easily attacked." But probably the best example she e-mailed me was a sign posted on a road in Kansai: "WEL COME TO JAPAN THE SEA MEN YOU GENTLEMEN DROP IN THE BAR KING AT GIRST: LADIES ARE READY. *In boxes and stands.*"

One day I heard Oscar announce: "Drink a note." I

asked him what he meant. He said in El Salvador people say "*Tome nota.*" In Spanish the verb *tomar* might be translated as either *take* or *drink*.

I mentioned this to the executive of the National Book Foundation, who happens to be a close friend. A great talker, he reacted by giving me several instances in which, while abroad, he had come across one restaurant menu after another that simply used dictionary terms without understanding them. For instance, in Port Bou, Spain, in 1979, he came across a dish called *Rape a la marinera.* This was a reference to monkfish (or angler-fish) in tomato sauce. He also remembers an item called *Rape, sailor-style.* Then he said that a non-English-speaking Catalan friend of his once came across an English-language learning manual from the twenties and forever afterwards used such phrases as *Dat's de cat's meow* and *Dat's de cat's pihamas.* Finally, he recounted the extent to which tourist expressions have embarrassed him—even though he sometimes had his own dictionary on the side. He was once in Jakarta. Just before going shopping, he looked up in the lexicon the word for *looking.* But when he made it to the store and a sales clerk asked him if he needed help, the word he looked up meant *searching.* He then mispronounced it, and it came out as, "No, thanks. I'm only stealing . . ."

It would be easy to ridicule Oscar's jargon but it would also be wrong. Embedded in that jargon are the linguistic structures he maneuvers in order to communicate in English. His language might sometimes be impure but it is never impractical. He is able to make himself understood far better than his mother Gladys.

> <

By far the most mystifying episode in Gladys's journey of assimilation took place in March 2004. It started in the early days of March. Gladys told me she had once again saved enough money to bring one of her children to the United States. Her daughter Fanny was already fifteen. Gladys hadn't seen her since she left El Salvador. Fanny and her sister Elizabeth were living with one of Gladys's siblings. Fanny is an average student. By all accounts she is also timid, perhaps even naïve. She isn't a big talker. Unlike Oscar, she also doesn't know any English. Gladys wanted Fanny to be with her and Oscar.

So she sent $4,000 to another coyote. Again, he promised three tries. Fanny left El Salvador on a Thursday. She was supposed to cross the Guatemala–Mexico border three days later and the United States–Mexico border one week after that. The trip was arranged so that Fanny would not go alone, but with a twenty-year-old cousin and her five-year-old son.

Gladys asked the cousin to give Fanny a piece of paper with Gladys's telephone number. She said she would.

The path to Sonora, the northern Mexican state, was long. It took an entire month. The cousin kept Gladys informed of their whereabouts by using a phone card. She would always call at 10 p.m. Eastern Standard Time.

By mid-May the three were ready to cross the Rio Grande. Regrettably, they were stopped by the border patrol and sent back. They spend some more days in Ciudad Juárez. The cousin had some money. But judging from the telephone calls, the behavior of the five-year-old was becoming increasingly difficult. He missed his bed and friends. He wanted to go back home.

It is hard to know what transpired in the early hours on the morning of May 24. The day before the cousin had called Gladys to tell her they would attempt a second border-crossing at 5 a.m. the next day.

For the next twelve days Gladys didn't hear a single word. Her phone remained silent. Then she got a call from a relative living in Virginia. The cousin and her five-year-old were already there. But somehow Fanny had been left behind.

Gladys was shocked. How could Fanny not make it with them? The cousin told Gladys that, at a given juncture, the coyote asked people to run to a bus parked across a highway. They all did. It took them forty-five minutes to run across unseen by passing motorists. Then, when everyone was seated on the bus, another man came on and asked everyone to leave the bus. People complied—but not the cousin. Fanny asked her to come down, but the five-year-old just didn't want to move.

In retrospect, it was the right choice. Once everyone was off, the man sat in the driver's seat and drove the bus to a neighborhood in El Paso where the original coyote was waiting. The coyote arranged for an airplane ticket for the cousin and the child for the next day.

As it happens, the cousin never gave Fanny Gladys's telephone number. She also had no money left.

The cousin did say that the day before they separated, the coyote got them false IDs. By then, Fanny was upset and ready to go back home if necessary. When the coyote took a passport photograph and asked each and every one for their name, Fanny didn't want to use her real one. Instead, she said she was called Ramona Gladys Pérez Lozano—her mother's full name.

Three weeks went by. The real Gladys had not heard a word from her daughter. Nobody in El Salvador had heard from her either. Gladys kept on calling everyone she knew: relatives in Los Angeles and Virginia, an on-and-off cellular phone number the coyote had given her at some point.

I saw my friend Gladys at La Veracruzana one afternoon. She told me the entire story. "*Fanny no habla ni una sola palabra de inglés,* Ilan."

She also said she wished she could give her the dictionary I gave her for her birthday. "She'd probably use it far
more than I do."

The choice of her name on the ID was potentially
disastrous. My friend Gladys had benefited from a moratorium on undocumented Salvadoran laborers signed
by the presidents of the two countries after El Salvador
suffered a tragic earthquake that killed many people and
left many more homeless. But she and Oscar were back to
square one—illegal again—after the moratorium ended.
There was a remote possibility of filing for a Green Card
under special privileges, but the details of those privileges were lost in judicial fine print. It might take years
to sort out.

Fanny's disappearance pushed her mother to despair.
Ciudad Juárez is known as a town from hell, a drug-
trafficking center, filled with Maquiladoras, where young
girls, almost three hundred of them, have been kidnapped
and assassinated. Their dismembered bodies are disseminated throughout the Sonora desert, where the corrupt
Mexican police, whose complicity in the kidnappings is
undeniable, find them later in a state of decay.

Gladys could not sleep and lost a lot of weight. Would
her daughter be okay? Could someone be taking advantage
of her sexually? She called me at all hours of the day seeking advice. I posted a notice in a missing persons' Internet

web site. But everything needed to be done with extreme care. If the girl was found by the authorities on this side of the border, she would be sent back to El Salvador. If instead she had gone back to Mexico, her chances of survival were noticeably slimmer.

I told Gladys I was ready to take a plane to Phoenix and look for her. I didn't know what good this would do: Where would I start my search? To whom would I talk? Contacting the police was out of the question. But I knew Gladys would find some comfort in my suggestion. After all, she wasn't able to book a flight herself and go. Her English was insufficient. Maybe Oscar could go. But then again, he was undocumented. As for Gladys's siblings in town, they did everything they could, but they needed to work from dawn to dusk every day.

The whole affair was terribly emotional. Language and memory—what are we without them?

> <

Then, out of the blue, Fanny—aka Ramona Gladys Pérez Lozano—sent word from Ciudad Juárez to El Salvador that she was all right, in the home of a Good Samaritan. (As it turned out, it was a Mexican woman whose energy in the past few years has gone to help "disoriented *señoritas*" like Fanny). The Good Samaritan would try to cross her to the United States in a few days.

Was it a ploy? Gladys appeared full of joy. She wired $800 to Ciudad Juárez. And she talked to the Good Samaritan on the phone a number of times. Fanny was fine, she told Gladys, but she hardly ever spoke. *"Como si un gato le hubiera mordido la lengua,"* she said. It's a Mexican saying, though I've heard a similar expression in the United Kingdom: silent as if a cat ran away with her tongue.

When Gladys told me this, the next day, she laughed. "No cat would do it, Ilan. *¿Qué piensa?* She'll need that tongue. In this country you're a *donnadie*"—a nobody—"if you don't open your mouth."

Fanny crossed the border for the final time on June 28. This was done in an unlikely fashion. The Good Samaritan drove her by car. They showed their IDs to the customs officer. It turns out that the last name of the Good Samaritan is also Pérez. She told the officer Fanny was her daughter. Then the officer asked the girl: "Yes, *ella es mai moder.*"

Fanny is now living in Los Angeles with an uncle.

< 10 >

In the Land of Lost Words

"*Perdón*," I say. *Perdóneme . . .*"

It is 1996. Night has fallen. Murmurs of nervous expectation invade the air. In spite of the heavy rain, the theater, as anticipated, is filled to capacity. A syncopated dance of umbrellas concentrates around the entrance door. People in elegant suits run to escape getting soaked. Taxis stop half a block away. Vendors scream to make others aware of their merchandise.

A poor Indian woman—bronzed face, dressed in embroidered regalia à la Frida Kahlo—sits on the floor, right under the huge marquee, which protects the hordes from the rain. Her skin is wrinkled, her hair long and disheveled. She is breast-feeding her newborn. At her side, a teenage girl, her torso and inflated belly uncovered, is sound asleep, oblivious to the hoopla that surrounds her. The woman has an extended polychromatic poncho on top of the humid floor. Its edges are wet. People's shoes scuff dirt at it. Why doesn't she move to a dry spot?

On the poncho she has arranged a colorful display of

rag dolls, souvenirs, and local candy—sweet-and-spicy *Chamoy*, Chiclets, mango and guava lollipops, Japanese peanuts. The dolls are pure Mayan folklore, and, in a way, so is the woman herself, dressed up as if some theater producer had paid her to be a landmark, to remind people that Mexico's modernity is still unfinished business, that although the government lavishly promotes the idea that, as Octavio Paz put it once, "Mexico has finally joined the banquet of Western civilization," the truth is otherwise: a large portion of the population still cannot spell the word *yo*. I look at her, my umbrella in hand; then I'm pushed from behind, and I stumble and mess up even more of her colorful display.

"*Perdón*," I say again, moving the umbrella to the side, then folding it.

Too big a crowd, not enough space. The Mayan woman looks at me in anger. Her baby has begun to cry.

I apologize again and again. Why so many times? Are my apologies a way to relieve my class guilt? In truth, I never know how to behave in awkward situations such as this one. Is that why I left Mexico? I ask myself. No, the reasons are far more complex.

Or are they?

I try to place the candies and dolls back in some kind of order. The woman utters a certain sound, but the hullabaloo around us keeps me from understanding her.

"*Ine hup-ka . . .*"

I smile apologetically.

"*Ine hup-ka . . . ,*" she repeats. She then adds: "*No-Kim-Bah.*"

In Mayan dialect, I tell myself. Have I ever seen a Mayan dictionary? Is there one available anywhere? The baby is in need of comfort, but she won't let me go. She must come from Quintana Roo, I tell myself.

"*¿Una limuznita?*" Do I have a few pesos to spare? Ah, she finally switches to Spanish to make herself understood. But she mispronounces the Spanish word for alms: *limosna.* Is she aware of it? Stupid me. I should have known what she was after. I take out ten pesos.

"*Unos garapiñados, por favor,*" I say. She knows what I mean: a bag of caramelized peanuts. Complaisant, she folds the money and stores it near her breast. Keep the change, I tell her, although she isn't about to give me any. Ten pesos for a tiny bag of *garapiñados* is a fortune, but I'm satisfied. At least I will be spared more guilt.

I put the munchies in my jacket pocket and look up. The rain is still falling, albeit lightly. The marquee reads, "Teatro Silvia Pinal: *Cantando bajo la lluvia.*" My father's name is in gigantic, handsome letters, brightly illuminated, right in the public's eyes. His pride, I know, is immeasurable. This, after all, is Mexico's most expensive and expansive imitation of the Broadway musical, a lavish translation of *Singin' in the Rain,* but for the misbegotten. The Indian woman is now pulling my pants. "Mister," she says, "*mire por favor,* Mister!"

Why am I a *Mister* to her and not a *Señor?* After all, I was born and raised in Mexico, just like her. The clue is that I'm Caucasian, a Europeanized Mexican. To her I look like a *gringo.*

Why is the word spelled *gringo* and not *greengo?* The latter spelling gives away one of its epistemological roots: green go. The color green, as in dollar bill, is always on the go! It's an informal, offensive appellation used to refer to a white person from an English-speaking country, mostly used in the Spanish-language words, in Latin America in particular. It dates back to the nineteenth century and means foreign as well as foreigner. Or else, it is used to describe gibberish. Might its etymology come from *griego,* Greek?

Oh, I'm very sorry: I'm again stepping on her poncho. I make yet another gesture of excuse and quickly make my way through the door toward the restrooms, where I meet up with Alison and Joshua, who just turned five three weeks ago. We exchange a few passing sentences of excitement and proceed down a long corridor. A gentleman is waiting for us at a back entrance. He leads us to the main dressing room, where my father, facing a large mirror surrounded by naked bulbs, is expecting us. It is only then minutes before the curtain rises. He hugs each of us and begins to chat with my son, showing him half a dozen photographs, offering him a cookie, and unfolding a telegram. "Abrémele. Stop. *Mierda*. Stop. *Mucho amor*. Comma. Haydée de Lev. Stop." It is from a Costa Rican friend, he says.

Josh asks why.

"Why what?"

Why *mierda?* What does it mean? *Mierda* means *shit*. So why does she tell Abraham to shit? We all laugh. It's the kind of forced adult laughter that results when a child misreads a certain expression. "Well," my father muses. "Not really. *Mierda,* in this case, is an expression of good luck. (Okay, *mierda,* I tell myself. But why not *cagada?*) In her telegram Haydée is wishing me the best—just like saying in English, "'Break a leg.'"

"But why 'break a leg'?" Josh wonders.

"Theater people in New York use the expression to ward off bad omens," answers my father. "If anything bad is meant to happen, the saying is supposed to prevent it. But in Spanish we don't say, *'Rómpete una pierna.'* It sounds too strong, doesn't it? It's strong even in English. So we prefer to say, *mierda.*"

"*Mierda* . . ." My son is puzzled. He doesn't understand. "Is *mierda* bad?"

"No, my father finally answers. "I really don't know why. It's just a saying."

How do you explain superstition to a child? My wife looks at me, at a loss, but Josh, his mind ahead of ours, asks, "What's an omen?"

A theater assistant stops at the dressing-room door. "Second call. Be ready, Abraham." He is followed by a svelte lady. She is to show us the way to our seats. We say good-bye. "And break a leg," adds my son.

We walk back into the crowded auditorium and are seated in a privileged row. I look around: the theater is filled to capacity with a vast array of parents and children, uncles and in-laws and nieces and old folks, all members of Mexico's middle class. This is the beast that almost devoured you, I tell myself, and reiterate: It is a *modus vivendi* you might have perpetuated, had you stayed around.

Everyone is excited. A bombardment of radio announcements, TV spots, talk-show pitches, praise, and discount ticket prices has generated much, muuuuuuuuuuuuuuuuuuuuuch anticipation.

I look around some more: people smile, move nervously in their seats. Not only will the full play *Cantando bajo la lluvia* unfold tonight, with a Spanish-speaking Gene Kelly dancing with a real umbrella under real rain and a Donald O'Connor impersonator singing "Make 'Em Laugh" in translation, but Silvia Pinal, the theater's owner and the grand dame of the Mexican stage, will make a special appearance. She will deliver a speech *en persona* in honor of the stellar cast and producers of this, the longest-running musical in the Mexican capital, and will uncover a plaque, to be hung in the hallway, commemorating the three hundredth performance of the show. Plus, she will host a cocktail reception where the actors will mingle with the audience.

> <

I have planned my trip south of the Rio Grande so that I could be present tonight. Not that I'm anxious to see the play. My father has been bugging me to come from the United States. "I'm ready to quit," he tells me on the phone time and again. "Enough, I've done it too many times. But I'll stay until you, Alison, and Josh come. I really want you to see it." He pauses, seeking an explanation. "Don't be such a snob, Ilan. *No te hagas el pedante.* You'll enjoy it!" And so I book the tickets for this special performance. "It's dedicated to you three," my father says out loud at home before we get ready to drive to the theater.

The three of us sit quietly, I glance at Alison. She smiles back. *"¡Es fantástico!"* she says.

A tight-skirted lady comes onstage. The light allows the audience to recognize the set design. A replica of Grauman's Chinese Theater in Hollywood stands at the center.

It includes a red staircase and a fountain. To the left is a small silver screen on which the premiere of a pretend movie, *The Royal Rascals,* is supposed to open for Gene Kelly's musical. The whole show is supposed to take place in 1927. As I wonder how close this Mexican adaptation will be to the original, I notice the cheap, derivative quality of the design. It aspires to look like a Broadway show, but it is funky, in bad taste. Is the svelte lady now talking onstage the one who helped us find our seats? Enthusiastic applause. Wait, who is she? Did I miss something when we said hello? Am I lacking context? *"Bienvenidos, damas y caballeros,"* she proudly announces. "Welcome to this fabulous adaptation of the legendary musical based on the 1952 Metro-Goldwyn-Mayer movie."

I see her mouth move, but I've stopped listening. Or have I? Did she say that *Cantando bajo la lluvia* is an adaptation of an adaptation of an adaptation? Josh's view is blocked by a female head with a pompous hairdo. "Can I sit on your lap, Poppy?" he asks. I consent. The svelte beauty onstage continues, "Since its debut twelve months ago, the musical play has become Mexico's number-one hit. Soon you shall see an authentic limousine crossing the proscenium. And even more extraordinary, you shall witness a rainstorm right behind my back, a rainfall as torrential as any in the Lacandonian rain forest and as nasty as the one outside." Laughter.

"Is it true?" Josh asks. "Is it, Pop, is it? Will it really happen?"

On and on and on ... the lady doesn't stop her blah, blah, blah. "It's an honor to ..." and, again, blah, blah, blah.

Is *blah* included in the dictionary? To my surprise, it is. The word, it announces, is used in informal speech to substitute for actual words in contexts where they are felt to be too tedious or lengthy to give in full. So what's the difference with *yadda?* None whatsoever. Juan loves Maritza, Maritza loves Enrique, yadda yadda yadda. And why is it that the two words, blah and yadda, always appear as part of a triptych (blah blah blah and yadda yadda yadda) but never intertwined (blah yadda blah, or else yadda blah yadda)? Go figure.

"Before the action begins and for those of you in the audience for the first time—not many, eh?—I'm here to introduce a short audiovisual retrospective sponsored by the beloved actors' union. Surely you'll enjoy this jaunt through the history of Mexican musicals."

Oh G-d, how much longer will she talk? I look at Alison and say, "Have we finally landed in the kingdom of kitsch?"

I wonder how the dictionary describes the word *kitsch.* I do remember, though, that Clement Greenberg, one of the early theoreticians of kitsch (along with my hero, Walter Benjamin), defined it as "vicarious experience and

faked sensation." Does that resemble a dictionary definition? No, it's too partisan, maybe even too thoughtful. But
aren't lexicons supposed to be thoughtful?

I like the early twentieth-century German word *kitsch:*
somehow, its sound invoked to me the phoniness of the
whole experience I'm part of. In German it is derived from
kitschen, "to throw together (a work of art)."

Alison laughs; so I do. The whole spectacle is unbeliev-
ably cheesy. Actually, not cheesy but cheeeeeeeeeeeeeesy:
exaggerated, overdone—in a word, theatrical.

Is there a Spanish equivalent for *kitsch? Cursi* is perhaps
the closest term, but it means "corny, overly sentimental."
Kitsch is different. It is more extreme. *The New Oxford
American Dictionary* defines it as "art, objects or design
considered to be in poor taste because of excessive garish-
ness or sentimentality, but sometimes appreciated in an
ironic or knowing way." The *Encanta* is less polite, though:
it defines kitsch as "artistic vulgarity" and as "tastelessness
and ostentations in any of the arts." And then, to crown
its message, it gives a single example: "tourist shops full of
kitsch."

Mexican-street Spanish, I swiftly remember, has an even
better term than *kitsch,* one that illustrates the complexity of the nation's culture: *rascuachismo*. Over the past
few years I've been infatuated with *rascuachismo.* I've
written about it in a number of places, including my auto-

biography *On Borrowed Words.* I've also discussed it in an essay about the legacy of the old-time Hispanic comedian Cantinflas in this context. I've gone to pains to explain it in English: funky, spunky, bawdy … but maybe there is more to it than those three words. I realize I have trouble defining it because concepts of such complexity are often beyond sheer words: we understand them emotionally, not intellectually.

Although *rascuache* emerges in the lower strata of society, it is a product of the middle class, which injects it with pride and self-respect.

How come the *OED* has no mention to it? Ah, because of its Anglophilia. Hispanic culture, until recently, has held a marginal presence in it. But the millions of Latinos in the United States are pushing the balance in the opposite direction. How much longer will *rascuache* be exiled from it?

Rascuache are porcelain replicas of crying clowns and slim ballerinas sold at Wal-Mart; the songs of balladist Juan Gabriel and the adolescent music group Menudo; the imitations of Yves Saint Laurent, Ralph Lauren, and Nike clothing; the comic strips of Kalimán and Condorito; popular comedians like La India María and Tin-Tán and wrestlers like El Santo; Mexican soda like Chaparritas and Tehuacán; and Chiclets and tamarind candy.

And how do I feel about *rascuache?* Closer than I would dare to confess. I grew up in a Jewish ghetto, proud of its European idiosyncrasy, refusing at all costs to give in to the arresting embrace of *rascuachismo*. But I now realize it was a lost battle. Is there anything more *rascuache* than the speech I'm listening to now—a celebration of the counterfeit—and my father's total submission to this sensibility?

Deep inside, I'm torn by ambivalence. While I lived in Ciudad de México, I despised its second-rate culture. But after years in the United States, I realize that as a term *rascuachismo* has enormous charm. *¡Es muy charmin'!* Authenticity isn't what makes it work, but to me it feels immensely more authentic, more Mexican, than the folkloric items—obsidian chessboards, key chains with an Aztec stone calendar, *amate* drawings of peasants plowing—sold to tourists in souvenir shops. Would dictionaries ever reflect these contradictions, what one sees and what one feels?

Yet I cannot but feel uncomfortable when it is so nakedly exposed. It forces me to ask: Is this me? Am I part of it? Or did I find a way to escape it, to appreciate it only from afar?

A background projector emits the first of many—how many?—color slides, accompanied by catchy melodies on a soundtrack than runs unsynchronized for about a minute and a half. The first image is of *Mi bella dama*. Reminiscing, the svelte announcer tells a couple of anecdotes about the production of *My Fair Lady* and its leading actress, Julisa, who is said to oscillate between the sweetness of Audrey Hepburn and the vocal stamina of Barbra Streisand. "We were all mesmerized by you, Julisa, weren't we?" she catechizes, and consenting yeses follow. Next come slides from *Godspell* and *Carousel* and *A Chorus Line* and what have you. My wife and son are impatient, but I'm having a ball reflecting on the event's metamorphosis. This habitat may no longer be my own, but it is still deep in my bones. It is derivative, an offshoot, a hand-me-down, yet it is deliciously original in its unoriginality.

Unoriginality: the dictionary defines it as lacking in originality or creativity. But the definition is wrongheaded. *Unorginality* is the quality of second-rate originality.

In how many languages has *A Chorus Line* been performed? Dozens, to be sure, but in none other than its original American English, in its cradle, on its native soil, is it fully at home. Or is it? I keep asking, impatiently, what this is all about. In India, in Israel, in Taiwan, in Mexico, the restaging of the musical may be a shadow, a tracing of the original, but I feel much more attached to the sensibility of the counterfeit because of its ability to recolor. If anything, my view of originality is not of a creation *ex nihilo,* but for a re-creation. "Mexico has a distinguished musical tradition," the announcer continues, and I want to scream: it doesn't, really. It never did, and therein lies its true value. It always refurbishes what comes from abroad.

A thought: Could a monolingual dictionary be translated? Could we imagine the *OED* in Spanish—not an *Oxford Dictionary of Spanish*—but the *Oxford English Dictionary* itself in Spanish? Another thought: Could anyone make a musical based on a dictionary—*In the Land of Lost Words,* based on the *Diccionario de la lengua española?*

At this point a *shtetl* in czarist Russia, a barren and primitive yet enduring village, appears on the silver screen, and it takes the old man seated next to me only a second to whisper unassumingly, *"Violinista en el tejado"*—*Fiddler on the Roof.* "You're right," the announcer says, as if in response. "Our beloved Manolo Fábregas, may he rest in peace, delivered a most memorable Tevye the dairyman. We all laughed and cried with him, didn't we?" *Tevye der Milkhiker.* I'm hypnotized. No, I'm flabbergasted. I recall the sentence, "If you're meant to strike it rich, Pan Sholem Aleichem, you may as well stay at home with your slippers on, because good luck will find you there, too." Soon, as if to accompany the rhythms of my mind, the melody of "If I Were a Rich Man" plays loudly in the background, and the ecstatic audience fills in the lyrics. "Si *yo fuera rico, yallah yallah yaddah yaddah daaaaaah daaaaaah daaadaaah . . .*"

I recall attending Fábregas's performance at barely Bar Mitzvah age. The musical must have been a huge success among Mexican Jews, for I remember my parents and grandmothers and a galaxy of other relatives talking about it for an entire season. I'm sure I was brought to it not only once but several times. It was my maternal grandmother, Miriam Slomianski, aka Bobe Miriam, a wealthy widow, who paid for the tickets for all of us to go to the Teatro Manolo Fábregas. (Why do established Mexican actors spend their fortunes in building their own theaters simply to have them named after themselves? Can the human ego be that overblown? It's a silly set of questions, I know, but . . .) She thought we would all get a strong dose of *Yiddishkeit* by listening to an imposing Spanish-speaking actor portray Sholem Aleichem's mythical character in a way that recalls Anthony Quinn (a Mexican) in *Zorba the Greek* (a gringo?). I wasn't as attuned to the delicacies of translation then as I would later be, but even so it struck me as fanciful that a Gentile cast, led by Fábregas, the child of refugees of the Spanish Civil War, would talk about *dybbuks* and *shlimazels*. Could a goy infuse a performance with *Yiddishkeit?*

Dybbuk, by the way, is also unrecorded by the *OED.* And *Yiddishkeit?* I'm able to find it in Leo Rosten's *The Joys of Yiddish.*

Many years later my father would tell me that Fábregas, a good friend, might have been part Jewish, on his mother's side, even though she converted to Catholicism and distanced herself from the Jewish community. (Her name: Fanny Schiller.) This probably accounts for his desire to stage Tevye in Spanish, not to mention the enormous profitability of the enterprise. The Mexican Jewish community is not only well off but addicted to entertainment, particularly the kind that strolls around Jewish topics not too seriously, without really confronting them.

But Fábregas's Jewish sensibility stopped there. He might have used his mother's unexplored Jewishness to capitalize on this venture, but nothing else he ever did showed any serious commitment to her heritage: he didn't attend the High Holidays, was rarely seen among Jews, and—aside from *Violinista en el tejado,* staged in Mexico in 1974— never, to my knowledge, took up any Jewish themes in his work, so thoroughly assimilated was he. In fact, no one in the Mexican Jewish community ever considered him a member of it. Fábregas thought of himself as first and foremost *un mexicano hecho y derecho,* a full-fledged Mexican, and then, perhaps, a Spaniard. (He loved Iberian wine and bullfighting, *la tauromaquia.*) In my father's eyes—and thus in mine—he was first and foremost a goy, even a supergoy: *un goyazo.* As a friend used to joke, *"¿Fábregas judío? Pero por favor. Si es un goyazo hecho y derecho . . ."*

These days I think often of all those obscenities we used, such as *goyazo.* They are outside the dictionary.

This is because lexicons, while elastic, catalogue by attrition. They offer us words to define ourselves, to explore our identity. But they cannot include every improvised term—not even compendiums of slang. I'm an admirer of J. E. Lighter, editor of *The Random House Historical Dictionary of American Slang*. When the first two volumes came out, A–G and H–O, I ran to buy them. The offensive expressions parading through their pages are priceless, among them *hole* for anus and *lush* for heavy drinker. When do these expressions have the right to make it to a lexicon? Only after they are repeated enough times—and not only by the young—can they claim a place in daily parlance. They are statements of character.

So where did the magic of his Tevye come from? Watching this jewel of a novel adapted to the Mexican stage, I'm sure, gave me and my relatives a naïve sense of self-respect. The plight of the Jewish people, I was told, was not up for grabs. It was for everyone to appreciate and celebrate. Nobody talked to me about the mannerisms it inspired, about the cheap nostalgia, about how it metastasized into a sentimentality that had nothing to do with the nineteenth-century ordeal of the Jews under the anti-Semitic czar. Nobody bothered to contextualize it as a cleansed melodrama in which the American Jewish community reveled and through which it revised its roots *in der alter heim.* No, in Fábregas's pseudo-Yiddishized, stilted performance, Tevye was a communal hero, a Pancho Villa of sorts, not authentic but endearing, the kind of icon Mexicans simply wanted to hug.

T-e-v-y-e: in its Spanish version, T-e-b-i-e. What kind of last name is that? asked a goyish neighborhood kid I invited to come with us to the show. What does it mean? And what's the guy's first name? "It means nothing," I replied. Nothing. There are words that mean absolutely nothing, especially names. What does *Manolo* mean? Yes, one might go to a eponymic dictionary (e.g., a dictionary of proper names), but would that change anything? To be truthful, the name is Tevel. Tuvia among Spanish-speaking Jews. Tevye is just a common diminutive, like Juanito and Rosita.

> <

Whoosh . . . I come back to my senses. The svelte lady is gone. Where did she go? I quickly realize that *Cantando bajo la lluvia* has finally begun. Kitsch is now tangible. The character played by Donald O'Connor in the movie is onstage. He's right in the middle of "Make 'Em Laugh," the number in which O'Connor dances on top of a sofa and up and down a wall, making everyone chuckle. The song is in Spanish, though, and, true to the script, *me muero de risa*—I'm laughing my butt off:

Haz reir, haz reir
porque a todos les gusta reir.
Papá me dijo, sé un actor,
si es de comedia, mejor.

Vas a ser popular,
en las carpas serás estelar.
Yo sé que hacer Shakespeare es de mucho caché,
y los críticos te aplauden, pero y la papa, ¿qué?
En cambio, con un chiste tu los haces puré.
¡Haz reir, haz reir, haz reir!

I laugh so hard that my stomach hurts. ¡Viva el *rascua-chismo!* My wife is also in tears, set off no doubt by my rollicking, and so is my son. In fact, I'm crying. Is the play really that funny? No, it isn't. What makes me laugh is the nonsense of it all, the subtext, the loss in translation. A few scenes go by, and the O'Connor and Gene Kelly characters are immersed in a free-for-all elocutionary exercise. "Moses supposes his noses are roses, but Moses supposes erroneously ..." Except that Moisés in Spanish is tricky rhyme, and so it becomes Rosa:

Rosa no pasa la raza de arroces,
mas pasa la taza de arroz al ras.

Si rasa la taza de arroz que pasa Rosa,
no pasa la taza de rasa de más.

"Tongue snatcher." Have I ever defined myself as one? Yes, a thief of words. I learn other people's tongues, making them my own. Only because translation is unattainable in perfect form does it become a worthy pursuit. For where would we be in civilization without translation? It is everywhere: in politics and literature, on film, on TV and radio. Too frequently I find myself looking for equivalents of one culture in another: How to render in Spanish the titles of *The Turn of the Screw* and *The Skin of Our Teeth?*

I also browse through dictionaries stealing words in order to enhance my vocabulary. In particular, I peruse bilingual lexicons because these are the only artifacts that make me feel at home, in a home-away-from-home, so to speak.

My mind is on the loose again as I invoke the Yiddish rendition of *Hamlet,* which, on its title page, reads: *"Yber-gezedzt und farveseret"*—translated and improved. But ... whoosh again. Where am I? Ah, yes: my father's *rascuache* performance of *Cantando bajo la lluvia.* It seems fitting that the story is about the passage from silent films to talkies, that it takes place just as Al Jolson's *Jazz Singer* is reinventing Hollywood, making it a habitat where gesture and sound go hand in hand. The next logical step is to open new markets by dubbing the talkie into other languages, pushing it out of the English-speaking realm and into the Tower of Babel. Suddenly Luis Buñuel, the Spanish film director, comes to mind. In *My Last Sigh*, his autobiography, he mentions an experiment done in Hollywood in the forties in which the very same set was used to film a script of *Dracula* several times in different languages. Each version had a different cast: the English-language version had American actors, the German-language one a German cast, and so on. The exact same story, but instead of being dubbed, it was reenacted in another tongue and cultural flavor. (The best one, I understand, is *Drácula,* the Spanish rendition.) So I ask myself, which of them is the original and which the translation?

> *Rosa . . .*
> *Rosa . . .*
> *Rosa . . . hey!*

> *Arroz es arroz es arroz, dice Rosa.*
> *Al ras es al ras es al ras, dice Rosa.*
> *No quiere que reboses la taza de arroces,*
> *no puede haber de más, pues la rima es ras.*

And what if, as the next number, "Rosa" were sung in Yiddish?

Reisl . . .
Reisl . . .
Reisl . . . oy vey!

Or else, in English:

Rose is a rose is a rose.
There it goes, just your nose—
just as Rose for she knows . . .

I hear myself singing to the same tune:

Rascuache . . .
Shmalcuache . . .
A farkakte Cuache . . . oy vey!

Yes, I've moved to a dimension where words have no meaning, to the land of the lost words. How would "The Star-Spangled Banner" sound in Armenian or "Home on the Range" in Mandarin? How about *Mexicanos al grito de guerra,* Mexico's bellicose national anthem, in English?

A downpour falls onstage, and yeah, it's time for the theme song, *"Cantando bajo la lluvia."*

Josh is astonished.

"How do they do it, Pop?" he asks. "The water . . . how do they make it look like rain?"

I improvise a reply: they have a tank ready behind the curtain and when . . . ah, finally my father is onstage, triumphant, personifying a 1920s Hollywood director. Josh says to me in English, "Hey, Pop . . . you saw him already? It's Abraham." I have noticed him, yes. When we last saw my father, in the dressing room, he looked like a clown. But onstage he is in context, a fish in water. He carries a loudspeaker in his left hand and is wearing a scarf, shorts, and a leather jacket.

Soon I realize that he isn't really concentrating. He looks bored. He delivers his lines professionally, without mistake, emphasizing what needs to be emphasized, but I know my father very well: he is distracted, not quite present.

But is he lost?

He raises his eyes and looks for us in the audience. We must be hard to locate, three leaves in a forest of trees. But yes, he finds us. My wife chastely raises her hand to say hello. "Pop, Abraham saw us! I know he saw us!" From then on it's a game between us, a sweet, enchanting game—an escapade: Abraham pretends not to be Abraham, but every time he can, he smiles at us or winks or delivers a line right to us. Pan Abraham! Pan Sholem Aleichem!

Pan in Polish is an honorific title for a respectable male, like *Monsieur* in French. But *pan* is Spanish is bread. Mmmm . . .

The show is over. Almost two hours have gone by. I turn

around, expecting Josh to be asleep. Not only is he awake, but he is singing:

> I'm singin' in the rain,
> just singin' in the rain,
> what a wonderful feeling,
> I'm happy again.

In English, though. When did he learn the song? When the crowd moves, we make it back to the dressing room. I remember the caramelized peanuts I have in my pocket. I take them out and begin to chew. My father is taking off his costume. "Did you like it?" he asks Josh.

"Yeah . . ."

"*¿Y tú?*" he asks me.

How can I explain to him what I've gone through?

"Uff," I reply, and offer him a peanut. I think of Cantinflas and Tevye. The dressing-room window is open. Outside the rain has not ceased. Josh is playing with the umbrella. He accidentally opens it and strikes me in the eye.

Ayyy.

"*Perdón* . . . Pop! I didn't mean to do it! Are you okay? Silence. It hurts. *"Oy vey!"*

"Pop?"

"Yes, I'm okay."

"Ilan, what did you mean by 'uff'?" my father asks.

"Uff is uff . . ."

< 11 >

Keeping My Name

"You've ennobled the family name, Ilan," said my father to me recently.

I had just been awarded some prize or other and his pride was visible.

I didn't pay much attention to his pride. What interested me was his expression: "A good name"—how does one go about getting one?

And how much faster is a bad one obtained?

I had a close friend whose name, as a result of some immoral action he performed, was . . . well, as his mother put it, *al fondo del pozo,* in total shambles. Not his actual name. Born a Jew, he—let him be called Julián—had incautiously gotten a Gentile girl pregnant. Julián kept the affair secret for some time hoping she would agree to an abortion. She had been raised Catholic, though, and, as it became clear, she wasn't ready to give up the baby in any way. In the seventh month, my friend finally told his parents. His mother, a descendant of rabbis, was mortified. She made a scene and threatened to throw him out of the house. "You've denigrated us all," she shouted. "We've not only lost our *buen nombre* but also all remnants of honor. It was your forebears who entrusted upon us that honor. Look what you've done with it!"

Honor . . . it might be impossible to lose one's name, but it is fairly easy to dispense of one's honor.

Before the 1970s, for a woman to lose her virginity symbolized the loss of her honor—and her family's, too. (This plight is beautifully conveyed in a thousand literary books, including one that left a deep impression on me when I read it at the age of eighteen: Thomas Hardy's *Tess of the d'Urbervilles*.)

The word *honor* is exceedingly volatile, meaning different things to different people. It is also in constant mutation, changing its value from epoch to epoch. The *OED* defines it—in its British spelling, *honour*—as "high respect, esteem, or reverence, accorded to exalted worth or rank; deferential admiration or approbation. As felt or entertained in the mind of some person or thing." Once, when asked what *honor* was, Gustave Flaubert responded by saying that the word is often misquoted. "But he that filches from me my good name doth make me poor indeed." Yet he added: "One must always be concerned about one's own, and not greatly concerned about others."

Is that true?

Look around: honor is everywhere—in politics, business, education, art. Each civilization has its own understanding of it.

In Spanish culture, there is a difference between honor and *honra,* which, to the best of my knowledge, has no equivalent in English. The *Diccionario del Español Actual* defines *honor* as *"cualidad moral que lleva al recto cumplimiento del deber y que hace a quien la posee acreedor al respeto de los demás y de la propia estima."* Translation: a moral quality conducive to the fulfillment of duty and which results in the respect of others on the person that holds it and in self-esteem. On the other hand, *honra* is taken to mean *"manifestación de respeto y consideración hacia una persona especial como reconocimiento de sus méritos y cualidades."* Translation: The manifestation of respect and consideration toward a special person in recognition for the person's merits and qualities. In other words, the first is caused by the individual himself in lieu of his actions, whereas the second is a construct attached by society to that individual—i.e., a perception shaped by the outside.

At first sight, the difference might appear insignificant. Let me make it clear: it isn't. *Honra* is an ancient concept in the Hispanic world backdating at least to the Middle Ages in the Iberian Peninsula. It is intimately linked with the idea of *limpieza de sangre,* purity of blood. In the process of *Reconquista,* Jews and Muslims were forced to convert to Catholicism. Those that refused were expelled from Spanish soil. But there were others—*marranos* and *moriscos*—who pretended to convert, but in truth they kept their original faith in secret. The Inquisition went after the so-called hypocrites, describing them as "impure" and also *"sin honra."*

Hence, to be a member of a *familia honrada,* one needs to trace the genealogical tree to Old—e.g., true—Christian. A person might achieve an honorable position in life, yet his past be tarnished still.

That, at least, is the established meaning. Today *honra*—and especially its counterpart, *deshonra*—is taken to mean dishonesty (synonyms: disrespectable, untruthful, indecent), for which Spanish already has another word: *deshonestidad.*

Among the most sensible reflections I know about the concept of honor, and its ever-changing nature, is the one offered by Alexis de Tocqueville in *De la démocratie en Amérique.* To understand its implications it is crucial to be acquainted with Tocqueville's odyssey. He was not yet thirty and an inexperienced aristocratic French lawyer when he published his celebrated book in two volumes: the first appeared in 1835 (only 500 copies were printed initially), the second in 1840. The fact that an accidental tourist, a foreigner with a penchant for political insight, could provide such an astonishing portrait of an emerging nation is astonishing. And the achievement is all the more striking when one considers that the deed was accomplished in barely a couple of years. Tocqueville and his friend Gustave de Beaumont, a lawyer at the tribunal of Versailles, received authorization in 1831 for an eighteen-month leave from the Ministry of Justice. The leave was to last just a bit longer. They landed in Newport, Rhode Island, in May of that year. From upstate New York they traveled to the Great Lakes and Canada and thereafter to New England, Philadelphia, and Baltimore. Their journey continued from Ohio to the Mississippi, from Louisiana, the Carolinas, Virginia, and the District of Columbia. They never visited "the far beyond"—the Southwest, still in Mexican hands at the time. Tocqueville and Beaumont were back in Paris in April 1832 and Tocqueville's understanding of the *system pénitentiaire aux États-Unis et de son application en France,* his original topic of disquisition, was complete.

Tocqueville, it is clear from the tone he uses in *Democracy in America,* is the ultimate foreigner, a curious traveler desperately eager "to crack the code" of the remote land on which he has fastened his attention. This is what all foreigners with at least a limited dose of patience dream of achieving. But his insightful sensibility is no doubt superior.

In the second volume of his book, he includes a chapter

called "On Honor in the United States and in Democratic Societies." In it he states that "honor is nothing other than a particular rule based on a particular state that a people or class use to assign blame or praise." He also suggests that "the human race experiences certain permanent and general needs," he argues, "and these have given rise to moral laws. All men, in all times and places, have associated failure to observe these laws with the ideas of blame and shame. They refer to evading these laws as *doing wrong* and to obeying them as *doing right*."

Doing right, doing wrong . . . in Tocqueville's view, the views on honor in an aristocratic system are understood quite differently than in a democracy. In an aristocracy it is defined by class—like Plutarch, he relates honor to virtue—whereas in a democracy honor is the result of enterprise and adventurousness. In the Old Word, honor is also attainable by a member of the upper social crust ready to be distinguished among others. Across the Atlantic it is far more malleable and also within everyone's reach. But here it depends on public opinion, which, as the Frenchman puts it, sometimes "cannot see distinctly where blame and praise are to be bestowed and is therefore hesitant in issuing a decree."

Public opinion, aka "the circus." Who is in charge of it? And how does this opinion express itself? Is it through politicians? Or pop culture? (Marshall McLuhan said: "Today it is not the classroom nor the classics which are the models of eloquence, but the ad agencies.")

> <

In *The Life and Opinions of Tristram Shandy, Gentleman* by Laurence Sterne, it is said of Tristram's father that "His opinion ... was, that there was a strange kind of magick bias, which good or bad names, as he called them, irresistibly impress'd upon our character and conduct."

Almost everything in language can be translated—but not names. In fact, they are stuck ("unable to go further") in the language in which they are born.

And, mysteriously, they also contain in their essence the DNA of their designated owner. How often does one come upon an Isabelle who fits the name to a T? Or a Stanislaw? On the contrary, people are prone to express—mostly in discreet fashion—their perplexity when a William should have been a Thomas and a Jennifer a Lindsay.

It is part of ancient lore that in the Bible, the name of G-d was erased, disappeared, vanished. Instead, readers are offered alternatives, some of them acronyms: Yaveh, Adonai, Elohim. For names in general, and G-d's in particular, might fall into the wrong ear ... with tragic consequences.

Names, names ... in early 1991, before our second son Isaiah was born, Alison and I composed a list of possible names. Entries were hotly debated, then crossed out. We ended up with a couple of male possibilities, and a single female choice. I remember thinking then: whatever option we endorse, it shall define our child's life forever. Had he been a Daniel, Isaiah—named in *honor* of Isaiah Berlin— would have been quite a different person, wouldn't he? And what if he had been an Anya?

Five years earlier, when Joshua was born, I discovered the plethora of dictionaries of onomastics available for the average consumer. I also came across more serious etymo- logical lexicons of names.

Plus, around that time I fell in love with the *White Pages,* which, needless to say, is also a dictionary, one sub- stituting definitions for addresses and telephone numbers. (I once wrote about this indulgence of mine in the *Iowa Review.*)

I don't remember spending too much time with direc- tories when I was younger. Today, every time I have one in my hands, I invariably take more than the usual few minutes to find people and connections.

The town I live in is fairly small. This explains why my *White Pages* barely has 250 pages. This brevity makes it possible to exhaust its onomastic bank rather quickly. In contrast, when I lived in Manhattan, the *White Pages* was a voluminous book, almost as obese at Joyce's *Finnegans Wake.* Interesting facts emerge. For instance, the pages de- voted to the letter *S* are, for some strange reason, the most abundant. In fact, in my edition they range from 194 to 218—that is, almost 10 percent of the overall content. They start with S & S Equipment Rental and end with Szynal, Jan M. (Stavans is excluded, by the way). The possibilities between these two extremes appear to be infinite but they aren't. They contain 1,756 different variations of last names. Next year, after someone moves into town and someone else leaves or dies, the configuration will change.

How did all these people end up with last names that start with S? Yes, it is a parental choice, but our parents, just like us, are subjected to the hidden laws that govern every culture.

Among Christians, a sense of tradition establishes that a son might be named after his father. So a single family might have two, three, four Johns. Plus, fashion plays a role. When I was little, everybody had an aunt called Pearl. This is no longer the case.

And then there are the toponimical lexicons, those devoted to the science of place names. (*Toponimy* was formerly called *nomenclature*.) For the most part a map of Israel today still uses the same names found in the Bible. In Russia, urban centers such as St. Petersburg have changed their appellations throughout history depending on who was in power. In Mexico, places negotiate their aboriginal and European identity. And the United States, in which, according to Robert Louis Stevenson, "nomenclature is

[more] rich, poetical, humorous and picturesque [than anywhere else in the world]," the traveler might unexpectedly find himself in Ithaca and Paris, as well as in places improbably named such as Embarrass, Minnesota, and Best, Texas (population: 1). Mencken dedicates absorbing sections of *The American Language* to the endless toponimical possibilities to be found—and get lost—in the United States.

> <

Am I the only person uncomfortable with his name?

I've always felt somewhat detached from it. Ilan Stavans—who did I become because of this appellation? I'm less interested in what each word means than in their connection to who I am, or might be. Why am I not Daniel Lombardi? Or else Pinkhas Kahanovitch?

When I was little, I wanted to be an Ignacio. I dislike the name today, though. I also dreamed of being a Jonathan. The disassociation I experienced toward my own appellation was nothing less than pervasive. As a form of rebellion, I would sometimes fail to respond when people called my name.

In my early twenties, I dreamed of creating a multifaceted oeuvre à la Fernando Pessoa, made through heteronyms.

Over time, the disassociation has not ceased. Instead, it has grown more complex. Upon seeing my name in an advertisement, related to a public lecture, on a book jacket, I invariably wonder: Why am I trapped in this prison?

The more I live (or "let myself live": in Spanish, *me dejo vivir*) and people attach my name to my actions, the more I wish to escape, to be someone else, at least temporarily. This desire to escape has made me write a couple of detective novels as well as a number of stories under pseudonyms. In fact, I've created an entirely autonomous persona whose literary work (I find it astonishing) is the subject of doctoral dissertations. No one connects her—yes, it is a she—and Ilan Stavans.

Similarly, I've visualized myself as the protagonist of an adventure modeled after Pirandello's *One, No One, and One Hundred Thousand,* in which the protagonist reads his own obituary in the newspaper one morning. Rather than reporting the mistake, he decides to take a vacation from himself—to disappear. This enables him to see the world as if he were looking into a fish bowl, a bit like the character played by Jimmy Stewart in Frank Capra's *It's a Wonderful Life!,* a movie that makes me cry every time I watch it.

Wouldn't it be rewarding to be outside myself for a while? Or would it?

Some months ago, I arrived in Los Angeles to deliver a lecture. A driver was supposed to wait for me in the airport. I waited fifteen minutes before I used my cell phone to reach my host.

"But I thought the driver had already picked you up," she said.

I told her I was quietly stationed in such-and-such exit and that no one had approached me. She promised to look into the matter and report to me right away.

My cell phone rang a few minutes later. "Are you pulling my leg, Ilan? The driver is already on his way with you in the backseat."

"With me? But I'm at the airport . . ."

The exchange continued as I tried to convince her that I was still at the airport. Again, she said she would call the driver.

"I'll tell you what . . ." I said. "When you ring the driver's cell phone, ask him if you can please talk to me."

She giggled. "Okay."

I waited several more minutes, unable to make up my mind: Was the whole affair amusing or frightening? The phone finally rang again.

"Ilan, you won't believe this. The passenger asked to be dropped off not at the museum but at a McDonald's nearby. He said good-bye."

"So? I don't understand . . . but the service assures me that some other driver will pick you up in less than fifteen minutes. Sorry for all this. There must be a misunderstanding."

"Did he pay the bill?"

"No, Ilan. It's a limousine, not a taxi service. The bill is charged to the museum."

I made it to my engagement late.

I never found out who the other Ilan Stavans was, his whereabouts, his appearance. My host persuaded me that it was some stranger ready to take advantage of a limousine. Apparently the driver was waiting for me at the baggage claim, displaying a sign with my name on it. He was approached by an individual who identified himself as me.

The explanation is entirely plausible.

But my wicked mind thinks of other possibilities. What if there is another me out there, news of whom I'm only allowed to receive sporadically? Is my honor in his power? I never discovered the identity of the con artist. Should I have? What if at some point he decides to "go wild," so to speak, and usurp my own place in the world? Could he present himself at my house and pretend to be me? Would he do the same in front of my students?

In spite of the ambiguities I feel toward my name, thoughts like these prompt me to hold on fast to it.

< 12 >

Dr. Johnson's Visit

After you've made a final turn, the brown, three-storied Dutch Colonial house in the middle of the block is still somewhat hidden from view. Several massive trees—two of them pine—prevent the visitor from seeing it. It takes a stroll to find out that the driveway is almost on the other end, behind one of the pines. Across the street, a placid football field extends the color green for half a mile at least. This, after all, is a college town. The athletic facilities are amenable. But they live in harmony with nature. The house is in a lot that was once an orchard and to commemorate its past, a few years ago my wife Alison planted two orchard trees in the front yard.

The archives at the Jones Library establish that the house was built in 1905. It was originally owned by an archeologist and explorer, Professor Fred Lumis of Amherst College. (He appears to have been related to the American impressionist painter, Harriet Randall Lumis.) A wooden structure with a maid's room in the basement, it was built as a present for Lumis's wife. Over the years the various

tenants—not more than five—have made renovations and
additions. The original cost was the grand sum of $5,000.
I know this because shortly after we moved in, in 1993,
one of Lumis's children, a geologist who taught in Arizona
for years, knocked at the door and invited himself in. He
offered Alison the history of the place: how it took seven
months to build; the exacts types of preserves kept in the
wine cellar during World Wars I and II; the weekly ice de-
livery, which would be taken in through the kitchen door;
the place in the backyard where chicken were raised and
a milking cow was kept; the stupendous Japanese tree in
the yard is a Katsura *(Cercidiphyllum japonicum),* one of
less than a dozen in the entire region, probably brought to
town by his father from one of his Asian expeditions.

"It's a generous place," Lumis's son said. His grandmother died in one of the rooms on the second floor. He
was born in the adjacent one. His father, he said, died during an expedition to Alaska when he, Lumis's son, was in
his teens.

> <

Years later—eleven, to be precise—on a humid Tuesday afternoon, around 4:30, a 350-pound man arrived at our door,
uninvited, fatigued, his wig almost falling to one side.

James Boswell once described this man as benevolent

yet austere, easily amused and good humored, agreeable to ladies, kind, versed in Dutch, French, Greek, Italian, and Latin, and awkward at counting money. Others have invoked the adjective *Falstaffian.* Johnson was surely voluminous in every sense of the term.

"Does it ever rain here?" he asked. I didn't say a word. "You know well that when two Englishmen meet, their first talk is of the weather."

He looked as if he had just trekked across the state and, more immediately, climbed up the three steps leading to the porch. I opened the door and gazed at him with surprise. How on earth had he made it to this neck of the woods? Was it really Dr. Samuel Johnson —eponymous poet, author of a translation of Horace, *The State of Affairs in Lilliput,* and *The Life of Richard Savage,* the bottomless commentary on the plays of William Shakespeare, *The History Rasselas, Prince of Abyssinia,* responsible for prefaces to every significant English poet from Addison and Milton to Young and Gray, the lexicographer of *A Dictionary of the English Language,* and the subject of that most magnanimous of biographies, Boswell's *Life of Johnson,* almost as voluminous as the man himself? Why was he here, in America, the place he hated above all things (well, perhaps with the exception of France and Scotland)?

"Don't set up for what is called hospitality," he said

when he arrived, uninvited. "It is a waste of time, and a waste of money. You are eaten up, and not the more respected for your liberality."

He looked around and immediately complimented the Katsura. The tree, it should be noted, is taller than the house: approximately forty feet. Not to notice it would be the equivalent of . . . well, not noticing Johnson's arrival itself. The Katsura is, in fact, as tall as the bell tower in the town's church. I told my guest that although *Katsura* is a Japanese word, the tree is also found in China. Its leaves were gloriously bronze. In the fall they acquire apricot and orange colors. It is at this time of year when the tree distills a fragrance of burnt sugar. It thrives in moist, slightly acid soil. Katsura trees were first traded to this country in 1865, but grew in Japan for centuries before.

"Dear Sir, one day I perceived that I had suffered a paralytick stroke. My speech was taken from me. I had no pain, and so little dejection in that dreadful state, that I wondered at my own apathy, and considered that perhaps death itself, when it should come, would excite less horror that seemed then to attend it. I longed in those days for a tree like this, but not in London. In London a man stores his mind better than any where else. No place cures a man's vanity or arrogance so well. But trees like this one, you don't see them often times. Cure might have come faster, I trust."

I showed him the way in. He straight away walked around my house, exploring the kitchen, living room, climbing up the stairs to the second floor. He stopped to investigate objects he had never seen before. A telephone, for instance.

"What good does it do?" he asked.

I tried to explain the way a telephone functions but quickly found myself in trouble. "It's a device designed to connect the voice of people geographically apart."

"It's an impossibility."

"It is, indeed. But technology has made it available." I asked to be excused and went upstairs to my office. I opened the *OED: telephone,* "an instrument, apparatus or device for conveying sound to a distance." Mmm ... my definition was better, I thought. So I descended the staircase again to explain to Johnson that the Oxford dons were not more articulate.

I found him on the staircase already. Somehow I got the feeling that Johnson knew my own house as well as I did. Had he been here before? He was about to go to the third floor when I recommended he change his mind. The staircase from the second to the third floor is steep. In fact, as one opens the door in the hallway of the second floor, one gets the impression of entering a closet. The steps are decidedly narrow. Not enough space to move around. Plus, I always have books piled up on the steps, limiting even more the space to put one's feet. There is a banister. Still, Johnson's obesity wasn't insignificant. I feared he would stumble and fall down. So I recommended we stay in the living room or at least go have tea in the second-floor studio, near the fireplace. But he refused. He hadn't come this far just to be in another average living room, he announced.

"I hear you embarked on a dictionary yourself . . . ," he said as he climbed the staircase.

Oh, so that's why he had come for a visit! Was I in line for a reprimand?

I certainly didn't need another one. Since I started my work on Spanglish, I've been the target of growing animosity. People easily confuse the messenger with the message. A cadre of purists has been on my case, all present academics, of course. Do I also need someone to come from the past to give me a lesson? Well, if so it should have been someone I hold in less esteem. How about Noah Webster, who lived in Amherst, not too far away, but who strikes me as a bore? Webster had a fecund mind, but he was a plagiarist. He downloaded—to use the jargon of our day—much of Johnson's *Dictionary*, historical quotes included. Or how about Henry Louis Mencken, responsible for the admirable book, *The American Language*? Ouch, but Mencken was an anti-Semite who showed little interest in things Hispanic.

"The people of your time are too permissive." He seemed agitated. From our syncopated conversation, he appeared to know much about the current state of literacy in the world. He mentioned that the average American uses no more than 2,000 different words a day—and, according to a growing assortment of pessimists, the number is rapidly shrinking. "Worse than in my time," Johnson added.

I told him our age focused on images. Had he ever been to an airport?

"Airport?" The words seemed foreign. "A port made of air?"

I explained to him what an airport was, how graphics were everywhere to designate telephones, restaurants, restrooms, gates . . . but I sensed I was going too fast. A "Power Book"—he wouldn't know what that was either, although he might be charmed by the idea. I asked him.

"I don't know," he replied. "But have you ever seen a zebra?"

"Yes, a zebra."

I mentioned a book I had seen about Laurent Spinacuta's Grande Ménagerie in Versailles in 1775. This was an annual winter fair where tigers, monkeys, armadillos, ocelots, condors, and other exotic animals were displayed. Maybe even a zebra. I continued: "Is it white with black stripes or black with white stripes?"

Johnson smiled. I returned to my previous subject.

"Today even a child is able to find his way easily in an airport."

"A child wouldn't know his way into the labyrinth where the Minotaur lived."

"Yes, the Minotaur didn't speak the local parlance either. You might as well be a mythical creature."

I added that this isn't a tragic turn of events, though. Images are the stuff the universe is made of. And they are the enablers of thought, too.

I stood up and came closer to him. "It is just as well," I added, "because people never thought in any language. People just think in images."

To prove this point, I told him I remember having read years ago an author—fluent in Russian, French, and English—who, when asked in what language he thought, replied: "People don't move their lips when they think. It is only a certain type of illiterate person who moves his lips as he reads or ruminates.... Now and then a Russian phrase or an English phrase will form with the foam of the brainwave, but that's about all."

"But the explication is only possible through words," Johnson commented. "No society, no matter how advanced it might be, is able to live without this type of intercourse. What distinguishes humans from all other animals is the capacity to speak. And speech is thought: to speak is to articulate ideas, to inquire. The word *flower* is not a flower but a symbol, one that makes the mind invoke the seed-bearing part of a plant typically made of bright-colored petals and a green calyx. And the flower is commonly abused as the metaphor of beauty. How else on earth would the actual flower and the metaphysical concept of beauty be summoned if not through words?

"Dictionaries are like watches," he said. "The worst is better than none, and the best cannot be expected to go quite true."

He asked what Spanglish was. I was taken aback by the question. How could I explain to Johnson this hybrid tongue? Surely he would disagree with my premises.

But I got the feeling that disagreement was not what he was after. I showed him a copy of my book, *Spanglish: The Making of a New American Language*.

"Is it too presumptuous to ask you to look for yourself? I'm—how should I say? A bit intimidated, perhaps."

He browsed through the red book. I saw a gesture of disapproval build up in his face. "What you have done, however I may lament it, I have no pretense to resent, as it has not been injurious to me. I therefore breathe out one sigh more."

I proceeded to defend myself. "It does pertain to you, Doctor, if you allow me to say it. Spanglish, whether we like it or not, is an essential component of the English language. It has already had an effect. Words like *buckaroo*,

nacho, rodeo, none of which I assume you know the meaning of, originate in regions where people from what once
were Spanish colonies now live. They have not had access
to knowledge, at least not in the way you have. And the
majority has not the vaguest idea of what a self-taught education is. Their parlance is born out of necessity." I paused.
"Have you by any chance stopped in London of late? Have
you heard the so-called Sub-Colonials speak? Well then,
there you have it. Spanglish is also a concoction."

Johnson clearly wasn't pleased. He responded: "He who
thinks with more extent than another, will want words of
larger meaning."

Johnson paused to inspect the volume again. And again
I was terrified. He sighed then said: "... a few wild blun-
ders and risible absurdities, from which no work of such
multiplicity was ever free, may for a time furnish folly with
laughter. What is obvious is not always known, and what
is known is not always present. In this work, when it shall
be found that much is omitted, let it not be forgotten that
much likewise is performed."

It was June. My office was hot.

"What has brought you to these regions" I asked.

"Curiosity. Curiosity and a sense of deference."

"For what?"

"The fate of English and the fate of criticism."

"They are both joyful," I answered. "English is now in

the hands of what you, Dr. Johnson, in your day and age, might have described as uncivilized midgets."

I explained that since he died, in 1784, America had become a global power. I told him about jazz and hip-hop and about graffiti too.

"Graffiti . . ."

"Cities like London have become notebooks. People write on the wall today."

"They did in my time as well. Advertisements posted on street corners . . ."

"But graffiti is no advertisement. In fact, it is a rebellion against advertising."

He was silent. I wished I could take him out and expose him to a set of fine examples. Instead, I opened an illustrated book. It offered displays of major murals in Berlin. I felt his puzzlement. I was about to comment on graffiti artists being exhibited in snobby New York galleries, but I stopped.

His eyes were wide open.

"What does it mean?" he asked.

"It doesn't mean anything in the traditional way," I answered.

"Everything needs to mean something."

"Well, then it means the end of meaning."

"You aren't a Scot! You're an American." Johnson uttered the last adjective with a decisively demeaning tone.

"Indeed, I'm not." I explained that I'm not even a native-breed American. "I'm a Mexican. Or else, a Mexican-American. Or even better, Jewish-Mexican-American."

He looked at me with suspicion. He disliked hyphenated words all right, but then what did *Mexican* mean? He had never heard the word, he said. I referred him to the kingdom of New Spain and talked about Florida, Colorado, Arizona.... These words were vaguely familiar to him, but not truly part of his active vocabulary. And *Jewish?* Ah, ah, ah ... "The Jews lived in London," he reflected. Then he sighed. "They were expelled ..." He then talked of Shakespeare's *The Merchant of Venice.*

Johnson sat on the comfortable green sofa. I asked him how was it that, according to him, a particular language came to be: "It must have come by inspiration," he answered. "A thousand, nay, a million children could not invent a language ..."

I told him the parable of the monkeys left alone with typewriters in their cages. At some point in time one of them was likely to type one of Shakespeare's plays, was he not?

He laughed. "Inspiration seems to me to be necessary to give man the faculty of speech."

"Yes," I told him. "Even Montaigne said this about of the power of speech: 'If it is not natural, then it cannot be necessary.'"

We paused for a few seconds. "And criticism?" I said.

"Criticism is a study by which men grow important and formidable at very small expense," he said. "The power of invention has been conferred by nature upon few, and the labour of learning those sciences which may, by mere labour, be obtained is too great to be willingly endured; but every man can exert such judgment as he has upon the works of others; and he whom nature made weak, and idleness keeps ignorant, may yet support his vanity by the name of a critic."

"You're a cynic!" I responded.

"Aren't all critics?"

"Yes, criticism remains for the idle. It has acquired much more political clout, though. One can't be a critic divorced from the problems of humanity."

"Why not?"

"It's a responsibility."

"No. The critic is the only man whose triumph is without another's pain, and whose greatness does not use upon another's ruin."

I was dumbfounded. Johnson looked at me attentively. He noticed my glasses and asked about them. Did he ever wear any? I wondered. No, he never did. But he knew people in London that used them.

I recalled that the first vision lenses were invented by an Arabic physician, Ibn al Haytam al-Hazin, but they were not polished and turned into glasses until 1283 by an Italian glassmaker. Spinoza used to polish glasses for a living.

Johnson appeared to want to talk about the making of his own dictionary. It took him endless energy to accomplish the task. He said: "I found our speech copious without order, and energetick without rules: wherever I turned my view, there was perplexity to be disentangled, and confusion to be regulated. Having therefore no assistance but from general grammar I applied myself to the perusal of our writers; and nothing whatever might be used to ascertain or illustrate any word of phrase, accumulated in time the materials of a dictionary which, by degree, I reduced to method."

His last line made me shiver. "Yes," I responded. Almost three hundred years after Johnson's birth, the intellectual world has been obnoxiously specialized. People devote entire lives to know everything about the most minute portion of the universe. Thus, the approach of a lexicographer appears utterly foreign today. Who would want to be a maker of dictionaries? It would entail getting some fundamentals in place: jurisprudence, medicine, music, sociology, chemistry, cuisine, literature, and the fine arts . . . even magic and alchemy. Who can know that much? And for what purpose?

Johnson walked around the room inspecting books. He

made a passing comment on the disarray in which some books were kept, particularly near the staircase and on the far end of the room. He found a narrative in Yiddish by Sh. Y. Abramovitch: *Travels of Benjamin II*. I explained to him that the author's pen name is Mendele Mokher Sforim. Can you imagine being called "Mendele the Book Peddler"? The book, I said, was a tribute to *Don Quixote*. Did he ever read *Don Quixote of La Mancha*?

He knew it was a shabby Spanish novel. His contemporary Tobias Smollett had translated it with much hoopla.

"Yes, and without knowing a word of Spanish either," I said. I expressed my admiration for Cervantes's novel and equated, the way many have done, a handful of passages to *Hamlet*.

> My words fly up, my thoughts remain below:
> Words without thoughts never to heaven go.

He recognized it immediately. "It's Claudius in Act III, Scene iii."

I slowly led Johnson to my Cervantes shelf and showed him a bunch of other translations. "It has grown immensely with time," I said. "English was the first language into which it was translated. The translation was by Thomas Shelton. It appeared in 1612." I pointed to the versions by

Peter Motteux, Charles Jarvis, T. T. Shore, Johns Orsby, Robinson Smith, Samuel Putnam, J. M. Cohen, Burton Raffel, and Edith Grossman.

"Ah, a lady," he noticed.

"The first one to finally break the prison built by an exclusively male tradition."

Johnson didn't look pleased. "Cervantes juxtaposed awareness—the words should really be *awakeness*—and dreams."

I asked him about dreams. How should a dictionary define the word? I had memorized one: "the train of thought, images or fancies passing through the mind during sleep." But do they really pass through? I asked. Or is the mind the one that passes through?

Johnson liked my inversion. In his mind it was a tribute to freedom. He was interested in freedom, he said, because it was an illusory state of mind. "Are we ever truly free?" he asked. "Our voluntary actions are the precedent causes of good and evil, which they draw after them, and bring upon us."

He seemed to have gone into a train of thought he was preoccupied with. Whose freedom was it, ours or G-d's? He then talked about freedom and determinism, which he called *predeterminism.* "The predetermination of G-d's own will is so far from being the determining of ours, that it is distinctly the contrary; for supposing G-d to predetermine that I shall act freely; 'tis certain from hence, that my will is free from respect to G-d, and not predetermined."

When Johnson stopped, he turned around and noticed some of my dictionaries. I talked to Johnson about how our fundamental conceptions of speech differ from those of his time. We no longer see language as mere speech, I said. It is a social by-product and also a series of conventions. That is, language not only in the sounds but in the genuflections, the fashion codes, the subconscious messages hidden between and behind those sounds. Language is a system, then, in which the value of each element depends on the overall disposition of other elements on the chessboard.

Johnson asked me if I enjoyed composing the Spanglish lexicon.

"I did," I replied. "But I often felt like a thief."

He wanted me to explain. "Spanglish idioms remain mostly oral. By codifying them, I felt I was robbing the people on the street of their creation."

"Those people are in urgent need of being taught. They don't know what's good for them."

I told him his dictionary was the only one I knew that might be read from beginning to end. I asked him if composing it was, as he is said to have announced, dull.

"Yes, dictionary making is dull work."

"I have used your quotes as a map to my education,"

I explained. "The authors you most often quote, in descending order, are roughly Robert South, Isaac Walker, Shakespeare, Dryden, Locke, Milton, Pope, Swift . . . I've read them in that order. Dictionary making might have been a dull endeavor for you, but you should see what it has become: a discipline entirely kept by bureaucrats, people without a soul. They are paid to collect words, to catalogue and systematize them. But there is little in them that sparks a fire. Dictionaries themselves have become arid, dull, and insipid. I long for a time in lexicography when the dictionary maker was also an adventurer, one ready to go to far ends of the earth for a single prefix. That is no more."

Johnson was quiet.

"In my own dictionary," I said, "I've been mean-spirited. The examples I use—Alfred cheating on his wife, Antonio bullying people—are all based on real-life people."

He asked me if I felt regret. I said no. Doesn't the literature we produce in some ways stand as a revenge against the unpleasantness we've received from people?

He stood up. Impatience was winning him over. "You were the first doctor. They are all doctors now." I paused. "You know, dictionaries suffer from an incredible flaw."

He looked incredulous. "What's that?"

"They're asymmetrical. If you know the word you want defined, you look it up alphabetically. But what if it was the other way around? What if what you had was the answer to the question? For instance, take bat's shit."

"Bat's shit? You wouldn't find it in the dictionary. Those aren't appropriate words."

"I like cacophonies," I announced. I was ready to talk to him about swear words and improprieties in lexicons, but I stopped. "In this case I simply want to know the precise term for bat's shit. How do I look it up?"

"You don't."

"But you included *fart* and *turd* in your dictionary, which the overzealous Webster eradicated from his."

Johnson had had enough. He pulled up the ample mass that represented his body from the sofa, rearranged his wig, and announced he was ready to depart.

"Where're you going?"

"Your handicap, my friend, is that you seek greatness in past men. But look at me. This gloomy tranquility which some call fortitude, and others wisdom, is but submission. Sooner or later we all learn that there are countries less bleak and barren than our own, that every man has his own ground, and that we have no choice but to endeavor to produce one's own labor. And you're infatuated with imitation. But all imitators are nothing but rigid censors. They seem to conclude that when they have disfigured the lines of he whom they imitate with some obsolete syllables, they have accomplished their design. Yes, the burden of the past is enormous on each of us, and it simply gets bigger every age. But every age deserves its own freedom."

Silence. He looked out the window. Far in the distance, behind a pine tree, he saw the football field. He asked about rugby. I said it was a different sport, far more brutal. He went out to the hallway and looked at the bathroom. I realized he had never seen a toilet and sink in his life. I showed him how to open the faucet. I pointed him to the toilet paper, explaining to him what it was. He was amazed.

"Even more amazing is the toilet-paper industry," I said. "Millions of dollars are made every year from it."

"Shit is money," he replied.

"And money is shit."

He descended the staircase by first putting his right hand on the banister. Halfway down, he turned around and said: "Whatever it is that you do, it is your duty. I had come to express my displeasure. And I have, indeed. But I see you won't take that displeasure to heart. This I applaud. Language changes, as you have well put it. Every so often I allow myself trips like this to sense the passing of times. I complain, as I have, but it is only because I am a begrudging old gentleman."

He was already on the second floor when I asked him one last question: "Have you heard of the word *logotheism?*"

No, he hadn't. Then he added as farewell: "I am, Sir, your affectionate servant."

I started to follow him. Johnson reached the front door, the same one he had used to come in. He exited and saw the Katsura. "You should consider it good luck to live under a canopy of leaves."

I smiled and blinked. As I opened my eyes again, Dr. Johnson was gone—an elephant of a man, whoosh, vanished like smoke.

< 13 >

The Impossible

In late 2003, I stumbled upon this death notice in the *New York Times*:

> An obituary on this page yesterday erroneously reported the death of Katherine Sergava, a dancer and actress who portrayed the dream-ballet version of Laurey, the heroine, in the original production of "Oklahoma!" Friends of hers reported the error yesterday.
>
> The obituary was based on one in The Daily Telegraph of London on Nov 29. The Times was unable to confirm her death independently and, through reporting and editing errors, omitted attribution. The Telegraph says it has begun its own inquiry.
>
> Ms. Sargava, who is 94 and has lived in Manhattan for many years, was hospitalized in November and is now in a nursing home.

The reporter caught Ms. Sargava "at the point of death" all right—but not quite there. The words death, dead, and dying are, in our vocabulary, ubiquitous. Take "Death came knocking at the door." Or "I'm dead serious!" Or else, "She's dying of boredom." And "The explorers reached a dead end, unfortunately." Also, "We've got her this time dead to rights."

The *OED* offers a long list of variants: *deathbed, death bird, death blow, death day, death fire, deathful, death hunter, death light, deathliness, deathling, death's face, death's head, death's herb, death's ring, deathward, death warrant, deathy. . . .*

I never heard of a bunch of these. *Deathful?* "Fraught with death." *Deathling?* Synonym: a mortal. *Deathy?* "Of the nature or character of death."

But what is that nature or character? What is death, exactly, for the lexicographer? In typical matter-of-factness, it is defined as "the final cessation of the vital functions of an animal or plant." Later on in the same column it slightly reconsiders its own approach, identifying death as "the state or condition of being without life, animation, or activity." Still, the definition is as blunt, even tedious, a definition as one is able to imagine. No fear is conveyed, no frustration. We die, don't we? Well, yes, but please let's get on with the business of life.

Wait, wait, wait! The final cessation, it says. So is there

life after death? What about reincarnation, or at the very least, transmigration? Well, these terms are themselves defined in their own section. But the definitions are not presented as redemptive: reincarnation is presented meagerly as "a fresh embodiment of a person," whereas transmigration is described in an earthly fashion as the "passage or removal from one place to another, esp. from one country to another." It suggests, as an example, "the removal of the Jews into captivity at Babylon."

Medieval and Renaissance lexicographers were less objective. They not only believed in salvation but actively encouraged their readers to trust themselves to the Almighty. But modernity has cured the endeavor of such excesses. If dictionary makers are said to profess a faith, it is faith based on the *logos,* the word—and not the word in general but in the written word. I would call such religion *logotheism,* the belief in the supreme power of words: nothing comes before them, nothing comes after. Words are their sole credo, for words are what make humans come alive and what justify people's existence.

So beyond and outside words, there's no palliative, I'm afraid! Go to the *Torah, Al-Qur'ān,* and *Bhagavad Gita* for answers. Go to an encyclopedia, even. Not to lexicons, though. They simply don't believe in an afterlife.

Or do they? I'm not convinced. We all, at some point, no matter how scientific a viewpoint we have, fear the end and look for answers. It would be absurd to think otherwise. We may try to hide that fear and procrastinate in seeking the answers, but it is unnatural not to have hopes. Hopes and doubts.

Ask Dr. Johnson! Did he believe in the benevolence of providence? The answer is characteristically ambiguous. In *The Rambler,* he wrote: "The great incentive to virtue is the reflection that we must die." But as is characteristic of him, in *A Dictionary of the English Language* he throws one equivocal remark after another. In defining one of the attributes of the verb *to sleep,* for instance, he states that it is like "to be dead," and then, "death being a state from which man will sometime awake." Elsewhere, he establishes: "There is nothing in the world more generally dreaded, and yet less to be feared, than death; indeed, for those unhappy men whose hopes terminate in this life, no wonder if the prospect of another seems terrible and amazing." Johnson quotes two lines by George Herbert:

> This hour is mine; if for the next I care, I grow too wide,
> And do encroach upon death's side.

So, does Dr. Johnson, this verbal wizard, believe or not in salvation? Once I imagined him coming for a visit. I guess I could have asked him in person. But I recommend not losing sleep trying to figure it out: in spite of a life devoted to definitions, Johnson was impenetrable to the core.

Truth is, Johnson is commonly known as "a man of the here and now"—a rationalist. I am one, too, but there's a difference. Don't ask me why, but I dislike the word *here*. To the extent that is possible in literature, I'll avoid it. Read my books: you will seldom find it.

Here denotes geographical location. The *OED* defines it thus: "in the place (country, region, etc.) where the person speaking is, or places himself." I perceive it as a form of imprisonment. Throughout my life I've rambled from place to place: Mexico, Argentina, France, Israel, England, Spain, northern Africa, the United States . . . but those wanderings are transitory. My true search has been for a place beyond place—in Spinoza's Latinate terminology, *sub specie aeternitatis*.

I also dislike the word *now*, whose coordinates are temporal and hence compliment those of here. *Now* is "at the present time or moment." Buddhism isn't the only religion preaching the "here and now." So does Judaism. The *Talmud* says that a single moment of enlightenment on this earth is worth more than a life in the thereafter.

Words aren't guilty of the emotions their concepts provoke in us. *Herein* and *now:* Why limit ourselves to the present time and space? The art that matters to me overcomes its own loci. It is with us, but also beyond us.

The word that single-handedly defines that geographical and temporal condition is *impossible.* For years I've been obsessed with this word.

Thomas Aquinas once suggested that the Almighty has power over everything except for the past. In his *Guide for the Perplexed,* Maimonides, indirectly responding to Aquinas, said that G-d exercises power over everything except the impossible.

But what *is* the impossible? I'm afraid to resort again to the *OED* because I fear it will grant me an uninspiring answer. And it does. *Impossible,* it states, in its typically long-winded fashion, is that which is not possible. It adds: "that cannot be done or effected," "that cannot exist or come into being," "that cannot be, in existing or specified circumstances."

In all honesty, I find no definition more unnerving. The impossible, it appears, is that which falls beyond the limits of the possible. Maimonides suggests that the impossible might be dreams, which I find quite attractive. G-d has power over us, but not over our imagination. The imagination is absolutely free, even from the domain of the divine. We can fantasize as openly as possible. It is all but a dream and doesn't exist.

Maybe the impossible is silence. I find this idea inspiring. Every word at our disposal has its own double: a nonword. Every dictionary that has ever produced a catalogue of words available to a particular group of people also creates its counterpart, a lexicon of unavailable words, words that are not possible, cannot be uttered, words that cannot exist or come into being.

Is this lexicon of impossible words a dictionary of silence?

Wouldn't it be fitting to seek the definition of silence and, yes, come across a vacuum, an empty page?

I open the *OED* in the letter *S* and look for *silence*. (By the way, why is it that the *S* demands more space than almost any other letter in the alphabet? Look at not only dictionaries but your telephone book, an orderly library shelf, the shopping list ...) So, what does the *OED* say? "The fact of abstaining or forbearing from speech or utterance (sometimes with reference to a particular matter)" and "the state or condition resulting from this." And then it states: "muteness, reticence, taciturnity." It also suggests that silence is repressed speech, that it is the cause of a compulsion to cease speaking on a particular occasion, and finally, that silence is proof that an argument has been overcome.

It still isn't clear to me, existentially, what silence is. Is it stillness? Is it absence? Stillness is an attribute of being. Absence, on the other hand, is the disappearance of being. Like most people, in my youth I loved sound—all kinds of sounds: speech, music, the noises heard in a sports arena. I love silence now: silence from my children's sighs and shrieks, my students debating a certain topic, a symphony by Brahms. As adulthood has settled in, I've become more attracted to silence. Silence is quietness. But at different ages in life it acquires distinguishing connotations. I remember that in my late teens, for instance, and also throughout my twenties, I was overwhelmed, as most people are, by a sense of immense possibility. I could do anything I wanted: study medicine, become a filmmaker in Hollywood, study Sufism and devote my life to the *Conference of the Birds,* join a circus in Kurdistan. Each and every one of these acts represented a path before me. Which one would I end up choosing? The piling up of my choices, I was fully aware, would eventually shape me as a person. But for the time being the choices were still there, unchosen. And each of these paths came also with its own sounds: a surgeon's instruments, the rolling of cameras, the quietude of a monastery, the juggling of bowls and roaring of lions.

Today I am who I am—in Aramaic, *eyeh asher eyeh.* Choices are still ahead of me, but I'm neither a doctor nor a mystic. I chose the path that excluded most others. Plus, in retrospect I realize that the choices I took were in the end less mine than I originally believe. They chose me as much as I chose them.

Mine are the sounds of a writer's life: a tickling keyboard, the student voices gathered in a classroom, a microphone magnifying my voice to a crowd, a TV camera....

The impossible for me is in the words that are not mine, the ones I'll never speak and write. The impossible is in the dreams I'll never have.

In Wellfleet, Massachusetts, almost at the tip of Cape Cod, where the summer months take me, I sometimes visit the grave of Edmund Wilson. Aside from my admiration for his crystalline, versatile oeuvre, I like the epitaph he chose for his tombstone to accompany him in death: *Hazak Hazak Venithazek.* In Hebrew it means: "Be strong, be strong, and be strengthened." In life, one must always seek strength to live up to accomplish one's purpose. But is the statement by Wilson, who by the way was an unredeemed skeptic, to be applied to life only? Is it also a recommendation for the journey that death represents?

What epitaph do I want on my own grave? And where will that grave be?

When I wrote *On Borrowed Words,* I included a series of paragraphs in which I envisioned my own funeral. But the editor believed them to be in poor taste and, furthermore, to add little to the overall narrative train. So I excised them—but not without a sense of loss. Today these paragraphs lay buried in my *genizah,* a secluded, spiderweb-filled closet where correspondence, manuscripts, photographs, and other memorabilia are stored. I looked for them recently, but didn't find them. I do know they came as corollary to chapter 2, "The Rise and Fall of Yiddish," in which I reflected on the diasporic makeup of my genealogical tree: my immediate ancestors went to Mexico from Poland and the Ukraine. And from Mexico, I migrated to the United States. Before and after these, for me as well as for everyone else in the family, is, figuratively, the Promised Land. I also remember invoking the turbulent harmony of Bloch's Violin Concerto in B Minor.

Maybe it's best that I didn't find the paragraphs. Maybe my editor was right. Who cares about one's own interment? That affair is not really for the dead but for the living. The bachelor Samson Carrasco imagined a most inane epitaph for Don Quixote:

> Here lies a strong-hearted nobleman,
> so wonderfully brave
> that even Death, opening the grave
> beneath him, could savor
> no triumph.
>
> The world never worried him;
> it thought him mad, it thought him wild,
> but he, like some innocent child,
> was granted God's mercy and mild
> forgiveness, and, living insane,
> he died like a man.

I wish for death—that cessation of finiteness—to come unannounced and for dying to be thundering and instantaneous. No reporters catching me at the point of death, please. I have no interest in seeing my whole life parade in front of me in a matter of seconds. What's done is done! But I do hope to be remembered for the care and devotion I gave to words. It was once said of John Ruskin that "he was one of the few Englishmen who, instead of tumbling out their sentences like so many portmanteaux, bags, rugs, and hat-boxes from an open railway van, seemed to take real delight in building them up, even in familiar conversation, so as to make each deliverance a work of art." Yes, words, oral and spoken, are an art within everyone's reach. But few take them to heart.

I have.

Does this make me a logotheist? Most certainly it does, and proudly so. And do I believe in an afterlife? Only insofar as it allows for a vision of Paradise as the place where language is no longer needed.

Dictionary: Say of it: "It's only for ignoramuses!"

GUSTAVE FLAUBERT
Dictionnaire des idées reçues, 1951

Acknowledgments

This book began in Ann Arbor, Michigan, of all places, in front of a microphone. I was literally asked to let my tongue meander for approximately twenty minutes dissecting any topic at will. I chose to speak about my life-long obsession with dictionaries. The talk was entitled "Ink, Inc." Delving into the gist of the two monosyllabic words, I explored the role ink plays in contemporary life, invoked its early Arabic and Chinese use, and moved into a meditation on the marketing of literature in the present age. My wholehearted gratitude goes to the organizers of the symposium, which was dedicated to commemorate the 25-year tenure of Laurence Goldstein as editor-in-chief of *Michigan Quarterly Review.* They were the ones who let the genie out of the bottle.

Fiona McCrae, publisher of Graywolf in St. Paul, Minnesota, was also a panelist. After my lecture, she approached me enthusiastically and, right then and there, encouraged me to turn "Ink, Inc."—soon to be an essay published in the *Massachusetts Review* (vol. XLV, no.10, Spring 2004:

7–15)—into a sustained meditation on dictionaries. The volume should be an autobiographical journey across language, she suggested. The epistemology of words should be my excuse. What role do dictionaries play in our lives? Who bestows the authority they emanate? And to what extent are they not only word books but depositories of collective memory?

She even had a ready-made title for me, one just perfect for the enterprise: *Dictionary Days.*

I was flattered but also frightened: Might such a brief rumination as the one I delivered in front of a live audience be turned into a book about definitions? At first I thought it was utterly impossible. But no sooner did I make it home than a different understanding became tangible to me. Whenever I open a dictionary, I often spend more time than I should or else than I thought I would originally commit. I not only look for the word I'm after but jump from one to another without constraint. I do so with a sense of utter freedom: I let the dictionary master my curiosity and not the other way around. In short, I am on the loose. So why not try to replicate that looseness?

A week later I e-mailed her a rotund yes. This, I thought, might be the most entertaining, as well as the most liberating, volume I ever embarked on. And it has been . . . somehow, words fell into place rather easily. Is it really possible to let the mind "wander and wonder" (the expression is by Langston Hughes) as loosely as I've done it in these pages? If the payoff is to be accused of bafflement, so be it. Literature ought to be as much about entertainment as about surprise. I'm guilty in equal measure of these excesses.

How does one become conversant in that most amorphous—shall I say labyrinthine?—of undertakings, lexicography? My objective, I soon realized, was not only to talk about words but about ... well, about the meaning of things in general. What is language? Where does it come from? What about silence—is it possible to define silence without resorting to the use of language? What are the connections between language and memory? How is the word *love* defined in the *Oxford English Dictionary* and in major lexicons used in other linguistic milieux? What about *death*—if death is the absence of life and life is in itself language, how might language refer to death?

How do dictionaries define words like *day?* Who makes these dictionaries? What gives them the authority to do it? What is the relationship between dictionaries and dreams? How is it that I learned to write because of lexicons? And what about the word *criticism,* which, for better or for worse, defines and encapsulates much of my life?

Finally, what would my revered idol, Samuel Johnson, say about *Dictionary Days?*

I offer no answers to these essential questions, only an analgesic to the existential ache that comes from taking them too seriously perhaps.

It is ironic that, having finally put the last dot in place, I find myself at a loss for words to thank Fiona McCrae for the invitation. I've also enjoyed the thoughtful conversations with, and excellent editorial advice from, the staff at Graywolf: Anne Czarniecki, Katie Dublinski, Janna Rademacher, and J. Robbins. The pleasures of working with a small press are enormous and I'm all the calmer, happier, and maybe even wiser as a result of them. The process of shaping a book is much more open and democratic: the author is invited to offers opinions in various areas, such as design, marketing, and publicity.

I wish to express my gratitude to my friend Margaret Sayers Peden for permission to reprint portions of her translation of Neruda's "Ode to the Dictionary" from *The Poetry of Pablo Neruda,* edited by Ilan Stavans (New York, 2003). And thanks to the Estate of T. S. Eliot for the lines from "East Coker," *Four Quartets,* Part 5 (New York, 1944). The stanza from Lewis Carroll's "Jabberwocky," part of *Through the Looking Glass,* is from *Alice's Complete Adventures in Wonderland* (New York, 1923). The verses from the *Al-Qur'ān* are translated by Ahmed Ali (Karachi, 1984). The lines from *Henry VI* and *Hamlet* are from *William Shakespeare: Complete Works,* edited by Stephen Orgel and

A. R. Braunmuller (New York, 2002). The lines from Lord Byron's *Don Juan* appear in the edition by Frank H. Ristine (New York, 1927). The dialogue by Johnson in the chapter "Dr. Johnson's Visit" is extracted verbatim from the *The Yale Edition of the Works of Samuel Johnson* (New Haven, 1958–). Samson Carrasco's epitaph for Don Quixote comes from Burton Raffel's *Don Quijote: A New Translation,* edited by Diana de Armas Wilson (New York, 1999). I made substantial use of *Words on Words* (Chicago, 2000), by David and Hilary Crystal. *The American Language* (New York, 1982) by H. L. Mencken was a fountain of inspiration. The quotations by Alexis de Tocqueville come from the Library of America edition of *Democracy in America* (New York, 2004). I used Jacques Barzun's abbreviated English-language version of Flaubert's *Dictionnaire des idées reçues* (New York, 1968). The translation of the first stanzas from "Deathfugue" is by John Felstiner from his book *Paul Celan: Poet, Survivor, Jew* (New Haven, 1995). The lyrics of *Singin' in the Rain* are from the two-disc DVD edition (Los Angeles, 2002). Used by permission. I also make reference to *The Lover's Tongue: A Merry Romp Through the Language of Love and Sex* (Toronto, 2003). I found useful Jonathon Green's *Chasing the Sun: Dictionary-Makers and the Dictionaries They Made* (New York, 1996), as well as the *Dictionary of Lexicography* (London, 1998), edited by R. R. K. Hartmann and Gregory James. Finally, the seed of chapter 6, "*Fictionary:* or, How I Learned to Write" appeared as "Writing with Verve" in *College Board,* No. 202, Spring 2004: 22–25. And chapter 10, "In the Country of Lost Words," was published in *Hopscotch,* Vol. 2, No. 2 (2000): 14–27.

Walter Benjamin once set himself the task of assembling a book made only of other people's quotations. To my chagrin, I realize I've stolen from him the endeavor. Ambrose Bierce, by the way, defined *quotation* thus: "the act of repeating erroneously the words of others. The words erroneously repeated."

ILAN STAVANS is the Lewis-Sebring Professor in Latin American and Latino Culture at Amherst College.

This book was typeset in Minion Pro, a typeface designed by Robert Slimbach and issued by Adobe in 1989.

Book design by Wendy Holdman. Composition by Stanton Publication Services, Inc. Manufactured by Maple Vail Book Manufacturing on acid-free paper.